Metal Clay for Beaders

Irina Miech

Acknowledgements:
I would like to thank Tony Miech for his constant support of my work, and Lauren Matusko for her writing advice.
I would also like to thank my wonderful store staff for their support, enthusiasm, and willingness to help in all my undertakings.

Printed in the United States of America

06 07 08 09 10 11 12 13 14 15 10 9 8 7 6 5 4 3 2 1

Publisher's Cataloging-In-Publication
(Prepared by The Donohue Group, Inc.)

Miech, Irina.
   Metal clay for beaders / Irina Miech.

   p. : ill. ; cm.
   ISBN: 0-87116-233-4

1. Precious metal clay. 2. Jewelry making. 3. Beads--Design and construction. 4. Silver jewelry. I. Title.

TT212 .M54 2006
739.27

Senior art director: Lisa Bergman
Book layout: Kristine Brightman
Consulting editor: Dori Olmesdahl
Project editor: Kristin Schneidler

Precious Metal Clay (PMC®) is a registered trademark of Mitsubishi Materials Corp., Japan. Art Clay® is a registered trademark of Aida Chemical Industries, Japan.

Photography by Bill Zuback and Jim Forbes unless otherwise indicated.

Introduction

A note from the author

Metal clay is an exciting innovation that's easy to use and very adaptable. You can mold, stamp, and shape this malleable material to almost any design you like. Then fire your creation – *voilà*! You have 99.9% pure silver jewelry!

I love being able to incorporate organic elements in my designs, and I am drawn to metal clay as a medium because of its unique ability to directly capture the beauty of nature. Its adaptability also works especially well for multimedia projects, which allows me to make one-of-a-kind components to enhance my beadwork. Best of all, metal clay lends itself to being used in many inventive ways—ways that I'm still exploring.

I began working with Precious Metal Clay (one of two brands of metal clay on the market—the other is Art Clay) in 2001, received my certification, and started teaching classes. Over the years, I've learned some helpful methods for working with metal clay, which you'll find in the pages that follow.

I wrote this book to appeal to two groups of jewelrymakers: beaders and metal-clay enthusiasts. This book is a primer for beginners who have never worked with metal clay before, but it also contains new ideas for those intermediate artists who have experimented with this marvelous new material.

In this book, you'll find projects to explore for each of the forms of metal clay, including lump clay, paste, sheet, and syringe. Each project starts out with step-by-step photographs and specific instructions; many include tips on working with metal clay, using specific tools, or creating variations on the projects. Each piece you create will increase your skill level and inspire you to branch off into other designs. For additional inspiration, each project chapter concludes with a gallery of pieces I've made using the techniques covered in the projects. By the time you finish this book, you'll have mastered several techniques and have the know-how and confidence to create your own unique pieces. Enjoy!

—*Irina Miech*

Contents

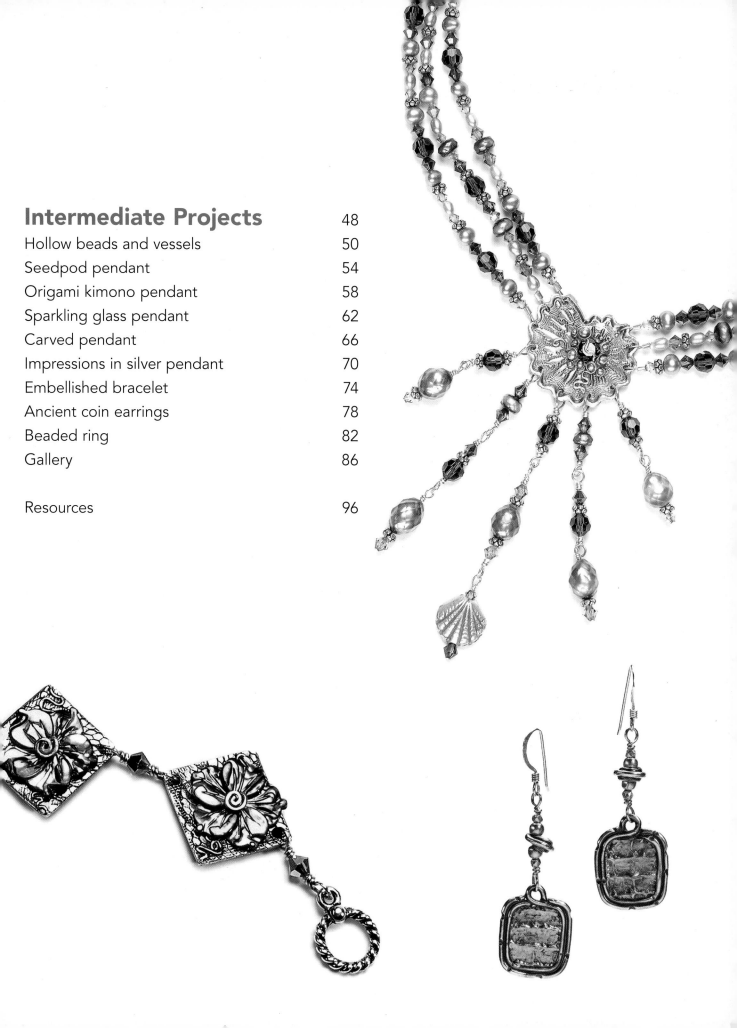

Intermediate Projects

Tools, Techniques, and Tips

Creating beautiful pieces of jewelry out of metal clay is a rewarding process. Inside this chapter you'll find a complete list of the tools you'll need to form and shape metal clay, as well as a list of the equipment needed to fire and finish your pieces.

Working with metal clay enables me to create silver jewelry without using the saws, soldering irons, and chemicals involved in traditional metalworking.

Photo by Tony Miech

METAL CLAY BASICS
What exactly is metal clay?

Metal clay is relatively new to the jewelry-making community, but has gained an ever-growing following in its first decade. This revolutionary material consists of small particles of precious metals—currently either silver or gold, though testing is underway for other metals—that are suspended in an organic binder. The binder gives metal clay its malleable elasticity; when fired, the organic element burns away, leaving 99.9% pure precious metal in its hardened form.

Two product lines are available to the artist—Precious Metal Clay (PMC) and Art Clay World. As a PMC Senior Teacher, I use PMC in my work, but both product lines are readily available, have similar properties, and come with complete firing directions.

Metal clay is available in four main forms: lump clay, syringe clay, paste, and sheet clay. See Resources, page 96, for sources you can use for metal clay products.

Lump Clay

The most common form of metal clay, lump clay can be rolled out into thin sheets, textured, imprinted, rolled into ropes, sculpted, or shaped by hand. Kiln-safe cubic zirconias (CZs), lab-created gemstones, and a few precious and semiprecious stones can be set into it and fired.

Lump clay has a low proportion of water in it and can dry out quickly, which makes it difficult to mold or manipulate if it has begun to harden. Keep unused portions covered with cling wrap and moisten the portion you're working with by periodically spraying it with a mister.

Syringe Clay

Syringe clay comes in a syringe applicator (hence its name). It is watered-down clay that is squeezed out and applied, much like using a cake-decorating tool. It is used to set stones and casting grain, and to create bails, lines, dots, spirals, and any other shape you can envision. Its possibilities are limitless, particularly if you have a steady hand. Syringes come prefilled and ready to use.

When using syringe clay, the best way to control it is to let ¼–½ in. [6mm-1.3cm)] of syringe "tail" dangle from the tip of the syringe and simply let it drop onto your piece, as opposed to trying to place it in a precise spot. You can always move it slightly with a damp paintbrush. The only time you hold the syringe directly over your piece is when making a dot or a blob.

Be sure to keep your open syringe's tip down in water whenever it is not in use; this will ensure it remains usable as long as possible before drying out.

Paste

Paste is clay mixed with water to the consistency of thick paint. It is used to paint on organic items such as leaves and pods to re-create them in metal. Paste is also used in conjunction with cork clay to create hollow beads and vessels. Paste can be purchased commercially or made by recycling leftover pieces of unfired metal clay.

To make paste, put your leftover pieces of clay into an airtight glass or plastic container (not metal) and add a little water. In just a few hours you will have paste. (If you add too much water and your paste is too thin, simply leave the container open and let the extra water evaporate.) Some metal-clay products are not compatible, so it's best to label the type of paste in a specific container.

Make the consistency of your paste fit your project. You can thin it by adding water; the resulting paste is commonly called slip and is often used as a "glue" to adhere pieces of unfired metal clay together.

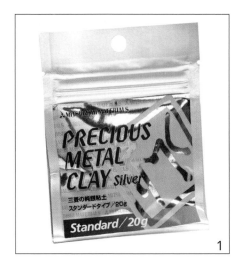

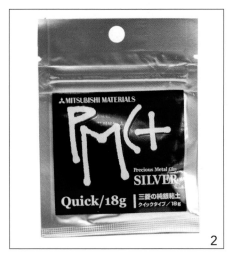

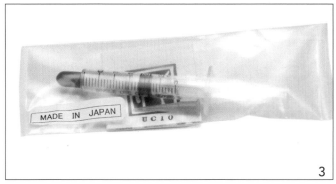

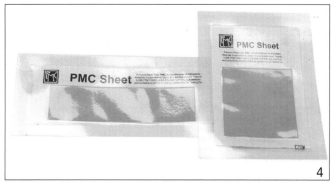

Sheet Clay

Unlike the other metal-clay products, which are water-based, sheet clay is oil-based. When you open its packaging, it doesn't dry out—which means you have unlimited working time. This product can be treated much like paper, and those readers who are scrapbookers will likely have a variety of paper punches that can be used with sheet clay. Originally intended for origami, it can be folded perfectly or cut with scissors to form intricate shapes.

Sheet clay does not stick to itself, so in order to construct pieces out of it, use Elmer's glue or syringe clay in small quantities. Avoid water, which can melt and distort sheet clay. If you must use paste, make it very thick to minimize the amount of water that can be absorbed.

PRECIOUS METAL CLAY PRODUCT LINE

The projects presented in this book are based on the PMC family (Art Clay World has similar products). The following is an

explanation of specific PMC products and their uses.

PMC Standard Products

PMC Standard metal clay is available in the lump form [1] only, which means its uses are limited because of the lack of compatible products within the PMC Standard line. Essentially, this means you will need to make your own PMC Standard paste and forego combining PMC Standard with syringe or sheet clay.

When fired, PMC Standard shrinks approximately 30% in volume—more than any other PMC (or Art Clay) product. The large amount of organic binder in PMC Standard and its correspondingly high shrinkage rate present both advantages and disadvantages. The biggest advantage to using PMC Standard is that it is well suited for projects involving carving. Its high quantity of binder makes this metal clay very easy to carve when dry, unlike other metal-clay products, which can be so brittle when dry that that they

crack or break during carving. This product is also an excellent choice when you are working with a busy design; when fired, the design will shrink to suitably intricate detail.

The disadvantage of using PMC Standard is its high rate of shrinkage, which is undesirable when exact sizing is important, such as in ring projects.

PMC+ Products

PMC+ products shrink by approximately 12% in volume. Because the shrinkage rate of this product line is lower, it's a good choice for projects where a minimal amount of shrinkage is desirable. It's available in the following forms:

• PMC+ lump clay [2] works well for any project requiring lump clay. The most important advantage of using this product is its compatibility with the other PMC+ products.

• PMC+ syringe clay [3] works well with any of the syringe techniques.

• PMC+ sheet clay [4] works well for all of the sheet techniques mentioned earlier. Even though all

5

6

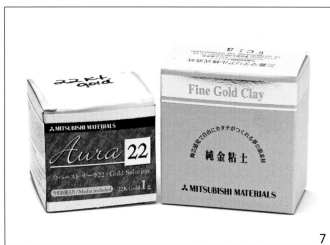

7

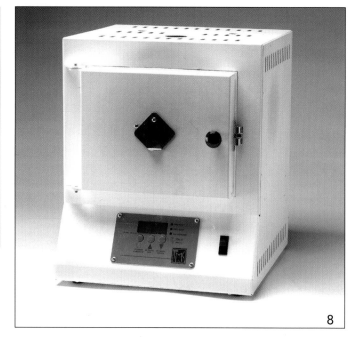

8

PMC+ products are compatible, don't use sheet clay with paste unless the paste has a very thick consistency, as water can destroy the structure of the sheet.

• PMC+ paste **[5]** works well as paste or as slip. If you make your own paste by recycling leftover clay or add pieces of clay to the commercially made paste, be sure to be consistent and only add PMC+ clay to this paste container. Label the container.

PMC3 Products

PMC3 is the best product to use for making rings because it is less porous than other metal-clay products; this means it's harder after firing and can withstand the heavy wear rings receive. Because the

PMC3 product line has a shrinkage rate of approximately 12% in volume, the same as the PMC+ line, you can use PMC3 products for the same types of projects as PMC+ products. You can even combine PMC3 with PMC+, as long as the finished piece is fired at the PMC+ temperature (which excludes the use of glass).

The primary difference between the two lines is that PMC3 products were developed as a low-fire metal clay, allowing them to accommodate the inclusion of dichroic glass in metal-clay projects. (Most natural gemstones can crack or even explode during firing, so lab-created cubic zirconias or premade, fused pieces of dichroic glass can be used instead.) PMC3 products are

tip

No kiln?

If you're not ready to invest in your own kiln yet, check with your local beading/jewelry stores. If they offer metal clay classes and have a kiln on the premises, they may be willing to fire your pieces for a small fee.

available in the following forms:

• PMC3 lump clay **[6, left]** works well with all clay techniques.

• PMC3 syringe clay **[6, right]** works well with all syringe techniques.

• PMC3 paste **[6, center]** works

METAL CLAY FIRING CHART

TYPE OF CLAY TEMP	FIRING TIME	FIRING (PERCENT) (MINUTES)	SHRINKAGE	FIRING METHOD
PMC3®	1290°F/700°C 1200°F/650°C 1110°F/600°C	10 20 45	10-12	Butane torch/programmable electric kiln
Aura 22® (22K gold)	1562°F/850°C 1472°F/800°C	10 30		Butane torch/programmable electric kiln
PMC Sheet® also known as PMC Paper	1650°F/900°C 1560°F/850°C 1472°F/800°C	10 20 30	Fire from cold kiln 10-15	Programmable electric kiln
PMC+®	1650°F/900°C 1560°F/850°C 1472°F/800°C	10 20 30	10-15	Programmable electric kiln
PMC® also known as PMC Standard	1650°F/900°C	2 hours	25-30	Programmable electric kiln
PMC Gold® 24K	1830°F/900C	2 hours	25-30	Butane torch (paste)/ programmable electric kiln

well as paste or slip. In addition, it is the best product to use for making repairs or for adding elements to already fired pieces.

PMC Gold Products

PMC24k gold clay **[7, right]** is available in lump form only. When fired, it yields a piece that is 24 karats—pure gold. Needless to say, it is not inexpensive! It is a little less pliable than PMC Standard, but it can be formed, imprinted, cut into shapes, and so on—just like the silver clays. The shrinkage rate is approximately 30%. It can be used by itself, or with any of the PMC silver products, though it must be fired first because of its high firing temperature, and then incorporated into the silver piece and fired again. Like the silver clays, it can also be used to make paste by adding water; see the project on page 78 for an example of this.

Aura 22 **[7, left]** is a liquid 22-karat gold paste that can be used to paint on fired and unfired metal-clay pieces. For a light gold, use one layer. For a darker gold, use two to three layers. Let it dry thoroughly between coats.

HOW TO FIRE METAL CLAY

Firing metal clay requires extreme heat to burn off the organic binder. This produces an unpleasant though nontoxic smell; adequate ventilation is recommended. Small pieces can be fired on a gas stovetop or in a portable ceramic kiln, but I find that the two methods below produce the best results.

electric kiln [8] The most expensive (about $500) piece of metal-clay equipment, a small, programmable, electric kiln will provide the most consistent results and is a must-have for anyone looking to sell pieces. Items that are fired in the kiln rest on a kiln shelf. Tongs are used to put items in the kiln if the kiln is preheated, and also to remove fired pieces from the kiln.

torch [9] Available at any

9

hardware store, an inexpensive (about $20) propane torch can be used to fire small pieces instead of a kiln. Make sure to use it in a well-ventilated area and to place the piece on a fireproof surface (such as a brick) when firing. To assure thorough firing, pieces fired with a torch should be 25g or less, and smaller than a silver dollar.

See the chart above to find out firing times and temperatures for the

10

11

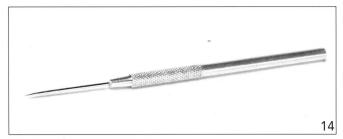

12

13

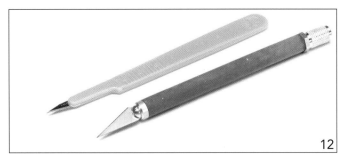

14

15

16

various PMC products. If you combine products that fire at different temperatures, make certain to fire the pieces at the higher temperature.

TOOLS

Although metal clay is relatively expensive, the tools you need to work with it are not. In fact, you may have many of the tools you need scattered around the house, perhaps in your kitchen, craft room, or garage. It's a good idea to round up all the tools you'll need for metal clay and then keep them together. Reserve any kitchen tools you use for metal-clay use only; to avoid contaminating food, don't return them to the kitchen.

Shaping Tools

These are the tools you will need for working with raw clay straight out of the package or for wet clay that is still being shaped or formed.

ball stylus [10] This is a shaping tool that can be used to create textures or to push down on clay in place of your finger to avoid leaving a fingerprint.

blending tool [11] Use this tool to blend seams in metal clay; it's also used to clean up debris on glass.

cutting tools [12] Use a craft knife, scalpel, or tissue blade to cut wet clay and to shape dry (unfired) clay.

greasing agent Any surface that touches metal clay must be lightly greased so that the metal clay won't stick to it. This includes the plastic mat and roller you use to start a project as well as any miscellaneous tools you use (such as straws for making bails). A natural hand emollient such as Badger Balm **[13]** works well, as does olive oil.

mister A mister delivers a fine, very thin layer of moisture to your pieces as you work on them. An old perfume atomizer works well (make sure to clean it thoroughly). Don't use an ordinary spray bottle; the force delivers too large of drops and can damage delicate pieces. You can also moisten pieces with a dampened paintbrush, but take care not to leave too much water in areas.

needle stylus [14] This tool is used to make small holes or to mark spots for later hole placement. It also works well to sign the back of your pieces. In a pinch, use a very sharp pencil in place of a stylus.

paintbrush [15] Small artists' brushes are used to apply water to clay. Dampen them to shape clay and syringe, to smooth surfaces, and to apply slip. Use them dry on newly sanded pieces to brush off debris.

paper towels A must to wipe your brushes on, paper towels are also great to wick away excess water if

17

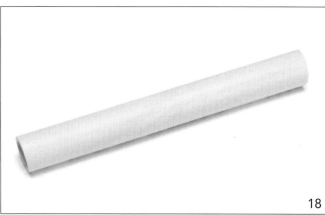

18

19

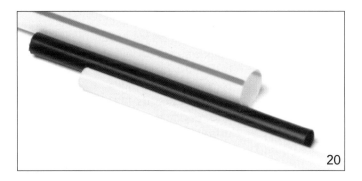

20

21

you accidentally put too much on your piece. Simply touch a corner of the towel to the wet portion and watch the water soak upward; avoid wiping your wet piece as you could mar the surface decoration.

plastic mat [16] Cut apart report covers (available from office supply stores or in the school-supply sections of other stores) to create plastic work mats. Always remember to lightly grease your plastic mat before you work on it. If you score your plastic mat in the process of cutting out metal-clay shapes, dispose of it and use a new mat—otherwise, scratches on the mat will transfer to the back of your piece.

playing cards [17] Metal clay artists and instructors use playing cards to control the thickness of a piece of clay that is rolled out. A standard width is three cards thick; you can tape sets of three cards together to make counting easier in projects that require many cards. Some projects will still require single cards.

roller [18] Used to smoothly roll out metal clay to a specific thickness (usually measured in a number of playing cards), a roller may be as simple as a piece of PVC pipe (available at hardware stores) or an acrylic brayer (available at art-supply stores). Grease it lightly before use.

ruler [19] Select a ruler that has both millimeters and inches, because both measuring systems are used in this book.

straws (assorted) [20] Small cocktail straws are used to create dainty bails, while drinking straws are used to form larger bails. Straws can also be used to punch holes in clay. It's good to have a wide assortment of straws, but bear in mind that since they come in various widths, you need to use the same straw when making components of the same size.

tweezers [21] This handy beauty aid is perfect for picking up and setting cubic zirconias and castng grain, as well as for removing leaves

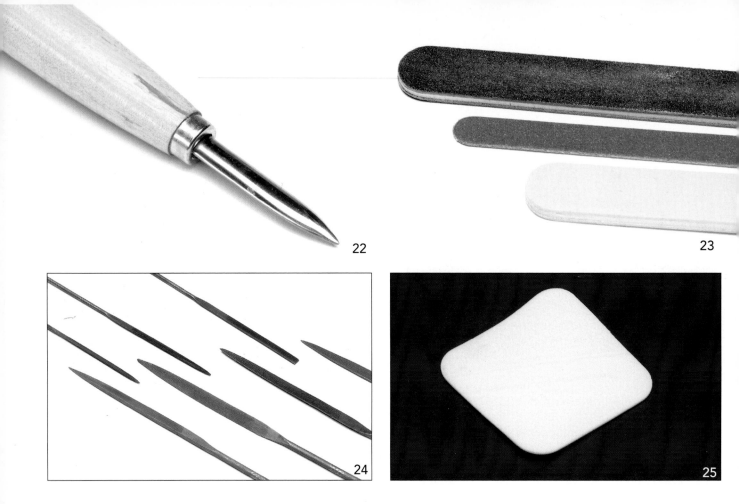

22

23

24

25

after imprinting them into metal clay. You can also use tweezers to remove fired pieces from a hot kiln, and to remove polished pieces from the magnetic polisher.

water Always keep a cup of water next to you while working with metal clay. Use it to wash and wet your brush, keep your syringe fresh, and add water to your paste if needed.

Finishing Tools

These tools are used to give metal clay a high level of finish, giving your creations a professional appearance. Some are used to refine a piece in the unfired stage, while others are used after firing. The more finishing you do in the unfired stage, the less you have to do after firing—and it is much easier to file or sand dry clay than hard metal!

burnisher [22] Burnishers are used to give a high polish to the high spots on your fired piece. The back of a spoon will also work as a burnisher, provided you don't need to get in any crevices.

emery boards [23] These handy and readily available beauty aids are used to file flat edges and surfaces of unfired metal clay.

liver of sulfur This unpleasant-smelling but nontoxic substance is used to give a patina or an antique finish to your fired pieces. It is available ready-to-use in liquid form,

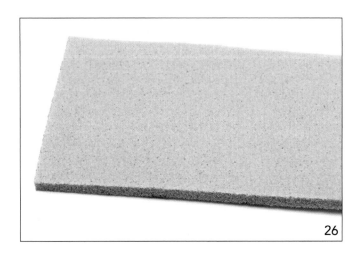

26

27

28

29

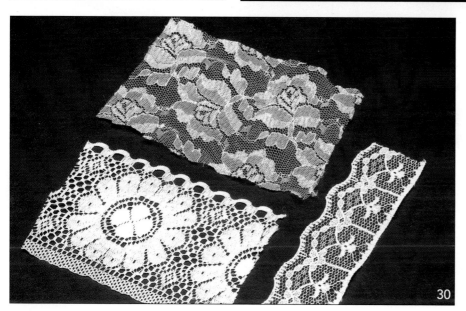

30

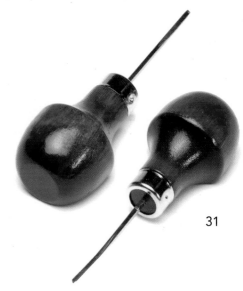

31

or you can buy the lump form and mix it with warm water.

metal files [24] These files may be used on either unfired or fired metal clay to smooth irregularly shaped areas or small crevices you cannot reach with an emery board or a sanding pad.

polishing pads [25] Used to remove most of the liver of sulfur, polishing pads leave the color only in the low spots of the piece.

sanding pads [26] Available in an assortment of grits, sanding pads are used to smooth three-dimensional, unfired pieces, such as vessels, beads, and rings.

steel brush [27] After firing, metal-clay pieces have a white finish to them. To give them a shiny metal finish, use a steel brush to scrub the pieces with soapy water. It may seem as though the brush is removing the white layer, but it actually flattens these metal particles, making the surface reflective.

Sunshine® cloths [28] These cloths are used to give a final polish to any fired piece, whether a patina has been applied or not.

Specific Project Tools

While most of the projects presented in this book can be made with the above shaping and finishing tools, a few of the projects require the following specific tools to ensure good results.

acrylic texture sheets [29, top], **brass plates [29, bottom]**, and **lace [30]** These items are used as texturing tools.

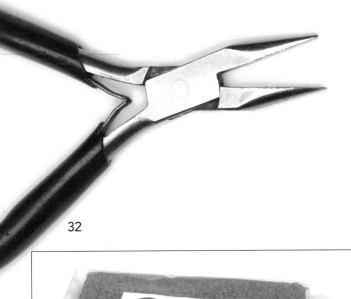

32

34

35

36

37

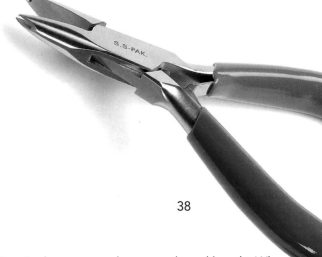

38

carving tools [31, page 15] These U- and V-shaped tools are primarily used with PMC Standard, because the high amount of binder present in this product makes it well suited to carving. Hold the carving tools at a slight angle and apply gentle pressure as you follow your designs. To make the design deeper, go over the carving again, removing more material. The carving tools are sharp, so exercise caution.

chainnose pliers [32] These pliers are used to shape wire. They vary from roundnose pliers in that they have angled jaws, useful for bending wire into right angles.

clay cutters [33] These cutters are used to punch specific shapes out of clay. They are used much like cookie cutters. You can use scrapbooking paper cutters for sheet clay as well.

cooking spray Ordinary cooking spray, such as Pam®, is used to lubricate rubber stamps to prevent metal clay from sticking to them.

cork clay [34] This substance is used to create hollow-form pieces, such as vessels and beads. When a piece that is made with cork clay is fired, the cork clay burns away, leaving the same shape in silver.

crimping pliers [35] These pliers have grooved jaws and are used to fold crimp beads or tubes around flexible beading wire, giving a professional finish to necklace and bracelet ends.

Elmer's® glue [36] Small quantities of Elmer's glue are used with PMC+ sheet to hold it in place.

HattieS Patties™ [37] These ring

33

39

40

41

42

forms are used to retain the shape and size of a ring while it is being fired; they are not reusable.

pencil Use a sharp No. 2 pencil to draw designs on dry PMC Standard prior to carving it. You can also draw lightly on PMC Sheet with a pencil.

prong-setting pliers [38] These specialized pliers are used to set stones and cubic zirconias (CZs) into a commercial prong setting. Hold the pliers in such a way that the groove straddles one of the prongs while the dimple in the pliers goes to the opposite prong. With the dimple part of the pliers, grab onto the prong and gently squeeze. The prong should move slightly. Change the position of the pliers so that the groove straddles the opposite prong (the prong that was just moved by the dimple part of the pliers); again, gently squeeze. Repeat this process with the opposite pair of prongs. Check if the stone is secure; if not, repeat the process again.

ring mandrel rests and straw rests [39] These rests are used to support your pieces so you can work on them without touching them directly and while they are drying. You can make yours out of two-part molding compound, which is formed into a round shape and then impressed with a round dowel-shaped object. Use a small amount to create a straw rest and a larger amount to create a ring mandrel rest.

roundnose pliers [40] These pliers are essential for shaping wire and creating loops, including wrapped loops (a common

43

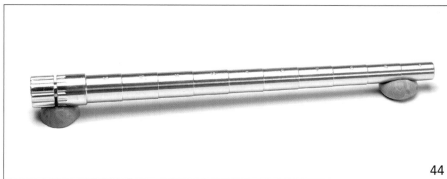

44

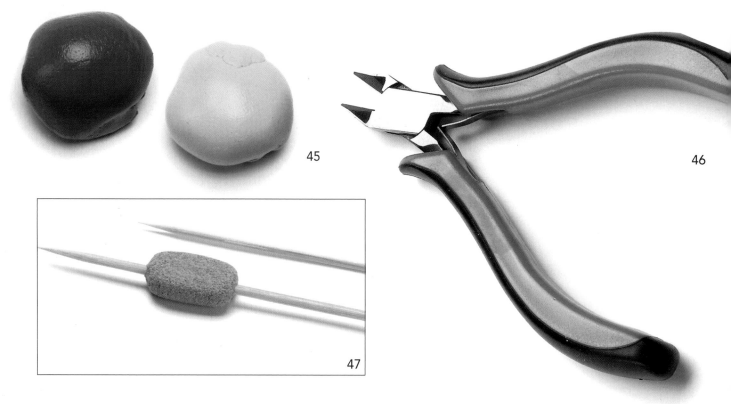

45

46

47

connecting device for adding components such as clasps to a piece). The round jaws ensure smooth curves to your wirework.

rubber stamps [41, page 17] Select stamps with strong lines to impress designs or images into clay; fine-lined, "photogravure" stamps produce poor results.

scissors [42, page 17] Sheet clay can be cut with scissors, provided they are small and sharp. You can also use patterned scissors.

split-ring pliers [43] These pliers, with one hooked jaw, make it easy to hold a split ring open while stringing on materials or adding a clasp.

step ring mandrel [44] This standard jewelry-making tool is used to form rings to the proper size.

tape When making rings, tape is used to cover the paper on which the ring is created.

toothpick A round cocktail toothpick can be used to create a very small bail.

two-part molding compound [45] Used to create molds, the two parts are mixed in equal amounts until a uniform color is reached. The object to be molded is pressed into the molding compound.

wire cutters [46] Wire cutters give a smooth-cut edge to the ends of jewelry wire. Look for quality wire cutters; the smoother the cut you make, the more professional your work appears. Flush cutters, a type of wire cutters, are used to make cuts close to the surface of a piece.

wood skewers [47] These inexpensive items are helpful in creating hollow beads and vessels; they can also be used for punching holes.

EQUIPMENT

In addition to the basic tools needed for shaping, cutting, and sanding metal clay, the following equipment is very useful for drying and finishing metal clay pieces. Costlier than the simple tools from the lists above, you may want to test this equipment before investing in it. The best way to do this is to take a metal-clay class (typically offered by your local community college or beading/jewelry-making shop); the instructor will have hotplates, kilns, tumblers, and more available for you to try during the class.

Drying Equipment

Metal clay needs to be thoroughly dry before it can be fired, otherwise moisture in the clay will cause cracks or even breaks to occur. The simplest way to dry pieces is to let them set overnight, but most artists don't have that kind of patience. You can hasten the drying time by using the following items.

food dehydrator Used for drying three-dimensional pieces; drying time may take 30 minutes or more, depending on the thickness of the clay and the complexity of the piece.

hotplate To ensure even drying of flat pieces, place them on this household appliance and turn them over occasionally. Most pieces will dry within 5–10 minutes. Look for a uniform light coloration—dark areas indicate moisture is still present, which could crack the piece if fired prematurely. A cup warmer makes an inexpensive drying device for one or two pieces, while a large griddle works well for many components.

Finishing Equipment

When metal clay is fired, it turns white. This layer is usually removed, although some people like this rustic look. Brushing the fired piece with a steel brush and soapy water will work, but if you want faster results, use one of the following devices.

rotary tumbler-polisher This tumbler polishes pieces with stainless-steel shot and polishing solution. Most pieces require no more than 30 minutes to achieve a high level of shine. Tumbling also further hardens metal-clay pieces, making them more durable. Delicate pieces, however, may break in the tumbling process, so take care.

magnetic polisher This device polishes pieces using polishing solution and stainless-steel polishing media. It provides a superior polish faster than a rotary tumbler by using polishing media, which are smaller than shot and able to get into tiny spaces for a more even polish.

METAL CLAY TIPS & TECHNIQUES

Keeping the clay moist

The lump form of metal clay dries out quickly, so make every effort to keep it moist and malleable. Remove only what you need from the package, and immediately wrap the remaining portion in cling wrap. Keep a mister handy while you're working with it, and spritz the clay from time to time to keep it fresh.

To keep syringe clay fresh, always store an opened syringe tip-down in a cup of water.

Rolling out the clay

To roll out metal clay, lightly grease a plastic mat and roller. Place the clay on the mat between two equal stacks of cards. If you wish, you may place an extra plastic mat over the clay to help it retain moisture. Be sure that the ends of the roller always rest on the cards, to ensure that the clay will be rolled out evenly.

Working with casting grain

Many metal clay pieces are embellished with casting grain. These little balls of precious metal are attached with syringe clay. Though I've used silver casting grain in this book, casting grain is available in other metals as well, including 24K gold, rose gold, and copper.

Handling with care

Once the clay has dried to a leather-hard state, it can be fragile. Work gently and carefully when filing, adding holes, and sanding.

Sanding

For professional results, use progressively finer-grit sandpaper (the higher the number, the finer the grit) rather than sanding the piece just once with fine-grit paper.

Do the majority of your sanding before firing the piece; leather-hard clay is much easier to sand than fired clay.

Adding a patina

Liver of sulfur can add a lovely antique finish or colorful shine to your metal clay pieces. It comes in two forms: dry chunks in a can or ready-to-use liquid. A little goes a long way, so buy a minimal quantity and use it sparingly. I like to use the dry form, as it stays fresher for a longer period of time.

Though liver of sulfur is nontoxic, its powerful, "rotten-egg" odor can be unpleasant. Be sure to use it in a well-ventilated room and avoid inhaling the fumes.

To add a patina, take a pea-sized chunk of liver of sulfur and place it in just enough hot water to cover your metal clay piece. When the liver of sulfur has melted, use tweezers to dip your piece in the solution. You'll be able to see colors appearing (the colors vary each time you make a patina solution). When the piece is a color that you like, remove it and rinse with cold running water. You can use a polishing cloth to remove some of the patina.

If you aren't happy with the results, you can re-fire the piece (in an electric kiln or with a torch) to remove the patina.

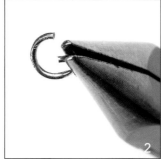

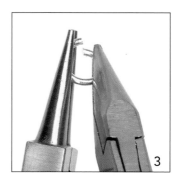

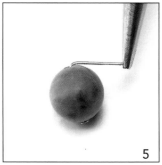

BEADING AND WIREWORK TECHNIQUES

A few simple skills are all that's needed to connect your metal clay pieces to ear wires, beaded strands, and more.

Opening a jump ring

This technique is also used to open plain loops, such as those on ear wires. Never open a loop or jump ring by unrolling it; this fatigues the metal.

1 Hold the jump ring with two pairs of chainnose pliers or chainnose and roundnose pliers, as shown.

2 To open the jump ring, bring one pair of pliers toward you and push the other pair away.

3 String materials on the open jump ring. Reverse the steps to close the jump ring.

Opening a split ring

4 Slide the hooked tip of split-ring pliers between the two overlapping wires. This ensures the ring remains open while you string on materials.

Making a plain loop

5 You will need at least ⅜ in. (1cm) of wire above the bead to make the loop. Use chainnose pliers to make a right-angle bend at what will become the bottom of the loop against the bead.

6 Grab the tip of the wire with roundnose pliers. Roll the wire to form a half circle and then release the wire.

7 Position the roundnose pliers in the loop again and continue rolling, forming a centered circle above the bead.

8 The finished loop will have a smooth, rounded shape.

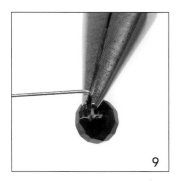  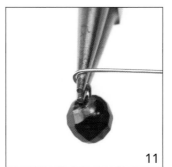 

   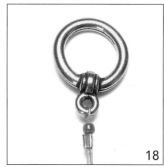

Making a wrapped loop

9 Trim the wire 1¼ in. (3.2cm) above the bead. With the tip of your chainnose pliers, grasp the wire directly above the bead. Use your fingers to bend the wire (above the pliers) into a right angle.

10 Position the jaws of your roundnose pliers in the bend.

11 Bring the wire over the top jaw of the roundnose pliers.

12 Reposition the pliers so the lower jaw fits snugly in the loop. Curve the wire downward around the bottom of the pliers. This is the first half of a wrapped loop.

13 Position the jaws of your chainnose pliers across the loop.

14 Wrap the wire around the wire stem, covering the stem between the loop and the top of the bead. Trim the excess wire and press the cut end close to the wraps with chainnose pliers.

Crimping

15 Position the crimp bead in the notch closest to the crimping pliers' handle.

16 Separate the wires and firmly squeeze the crimp.

17 Move the crimp into the notch at the pliers' tip and hold the crimp as shown. Squeeze the crimp bead, folding it in half at the indentation.

18 Tug the clasp to make sure the folded crimp is secure.

Beginner Projects

This chapter presents five basic projects that are terrific starting points for artists new to metal clay: two simple stamped pendants; a bracelet composed of textured links; a charming, organic pendant and earrings set; and a basic bead that's easy to embellish. You'll learn how to work with clay paste as well as lump and syringe clay. Mastery of these techniques will prepare you for the projects in the next chapter.

Stamped pendant

Use an unmounted stamp with the design of your choice to create a custom pendant. If you enjoy this technique, turn to page 43 for additional project ideas.

This stamped pendant is a wonderful project for beginners. The stamp provides the design, and you can add as little or as much embellishment as you choose. I like natural, organic themes, so I selected an ammonite stamp and added some casting grain for additional texture.

Be sure to choose an unmounted, regular-thickness (not extra-heavy) stamp.

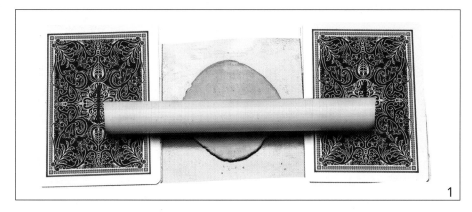

1

1-2 Grease your plastic mat and roller, then roll the clay out to a thickness of four cards **[1]**. Make sure the rolled-out piece is large enough to accommodate the image on the stamp **[2]**; leave extra space (about 15mm) at the top where the bail will be located.

3 Spray the stamp with cooking spray and remove excess oil with a paper towel. Add six cards to each side, so that you now have a total of 10 cards in each stack. Place the stamp on the clay, and roll over the stamp to imprint it into the clay. Make sure that your roller rests on the card stacks at all times; otherwise, it will distort the impression made by the stamp. Carefully remove the stamp **[3]**, using tweezers if necessary.

4-5 Using a craft knife or scalpel, trim the excess clay around the stamped impression,

2

3

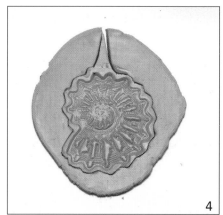

4

5

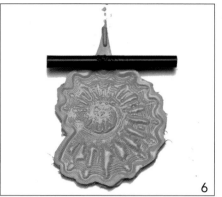

6

7

8

9

10

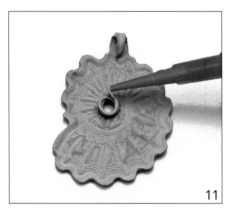

11

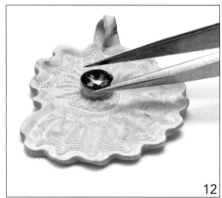

12

13

leaving a tapered wedge at least 15mm long for the bail **[4]**. Leave a 1–2mm margin around the impression as a lip or edge **[5]**.

6-7 To make the bail, liberally grease one of the straws. Place the straw at the base of the wedge that is intended for the bail **[6]**. Roll the tail of the wedge over the straw and put a drop of syringe clay on the underside of the tip of the wedge to adhere the clay where it touches **[7]**. Use a ball stylus to gently press the tip of the bail into place; do not use your fingertip to press, as it will leave an imprint.

8 Select a spot for the cubic zirconia (CZ); the stamp shown features a nice central location for a CZ. Using an ungreased cocktail straw, punch a hole in the spot **[8]**. Let the piece dry.

9 Once the piece has dried, remove the straw and use your emery board and metal files to file the edges and bail so that they are smooth and have no sharp edges **[9]**. If you wish, sign your piece on the back side with a needle stylus.

10-11 Using a clean brush and water, create a wet trail around the hole you

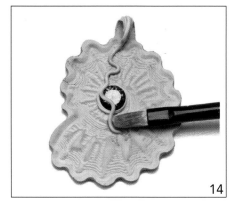

14

15

16

17

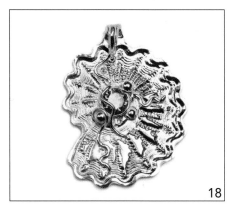

18

19

materials

- PMC+ or PMC3 lump clay
- PMC+ or PMC3 syringe clay
- casting grain
- 6mm kiln-safe cubic zirconia (CZ)
- Badger Balm or olive oil
- plastic mat
- roller
- 20 playing cards
- unmounted stamp (regular thickness, not extra-heavy)
- cooking spray
- paper towel
- tweezers
- craft knife or scalpel
- 2 cocktail straws
- ball stylus
- metal file or emery board
- needle stylus (optional)
- small brush
- water
- steel brush
- burnisher
- tumbler (optional)
- liver of sulfur (optional)

punched in step 8 **[10]**. The wetted clay helps the syringe clay attach to the rest of the piece. Take your syringe and apply enough pressure to create a 5–10mm tail. Create a two- to three-tiered well around the hole, letting the syringe drop into place instead of forcing it **[11]**. Place the brush in the opening of the well and push out the walls of the well by gently moving the brush in a circular motion. If necessary, the outer walls of the well can be pushed in gently.

12-14 Pick up the CZ with your tweezers and place it on top of the still-wet well **[12]**. Gently push the CZ in all the

way with your tweezers. Tap the surface of the CZ to settle it horizontally **[13]**. The edge of the well should be above the edge of the CZ. If it isn't, make a wet trail with your brush and then add a string of syringe clay across the surface of the CZ **[14]**; this will help keep the CZ secure after firing. If the string seems loose, attach it more firmly with a little more water.

15-17 Determine where you wish to add casting grain. Wet the desired spots with a brush, place your syringe above the area, and squeeze out a blob of clay approximately the same size as the

casting grain **[15]**. Pick up the casting grain with tweezers and place it on top of the syringe-clay blob. Use the end of the tweezers to gently push the casting grain all the way into the blob, which will create a bezel (or setting) for the grain **[16]**. Add more casting grain in the same manner and embellish the piece further with syringe if desired **[17]**. Dry the piece and fire according to the manufacturer's instructions.

18-19 Scrub the piece with a steel brush and polish it with a burnisher until the silver shines **[18]**. If you have a tumbler, you can use that instead. If you wish, use liver of sulfur to add a patina **[19]** as described on page 19.

Create a clean, crisp-looking pendant with a Celtic-themed stamp. If you enjoy this technique, turn to page 44 for additional project ideas.

I enjoy incorporating the beautiful, ancient themes of Celtic knotwork into my designs. The knotwork is rich in history, and its clean, crisp look requires little embellishment. I've found that using a prong setting for cubic zirconias works well with Celtic themes; a prong setting draws attention to the jewel without distracting from the intricate knotwork.

1 Grease your plastic mat and roller, then roll the clay out to the thickness of four to six cards [1]. (Five cards is the optimal thickness, but if you prefer a thinner or thicker pendant, vary the number of cards.) Make sure the piece of clay you rolled out is large enough to accommodate the stamp.

2 Spray the stamp with cooking spray and remove the excess oil with a paper towel. Add six cards to each stack (if you started with five cards, then you should have 11 cards on each side) and place the stamp on the clay. Roll over the stamp to imprint it in the clay, making sure that your roller rests on the card stacks at all times [2].

3 Carefully remove the stamp [3], using tweezers if necessary.

4 Determine the location of the cubic zirconia (CZ) and push the prong setting into the clay [4].

5 Leaving a 1–2mm margin around the edge of the impression and setting, trim the excess clay with a craft knife. As you trim, save a strip of clay at least 4mm wide and 15mm long for the bail [5, page 30].

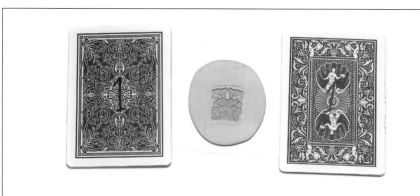

1

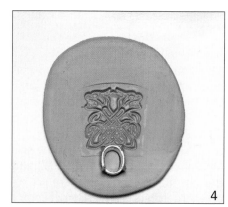

2

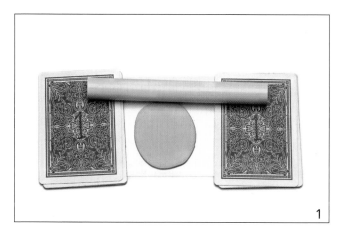

3

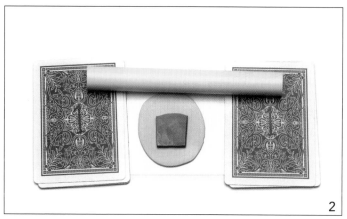

4

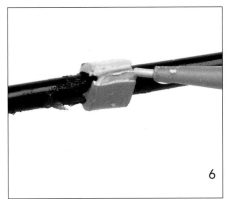

materials

- PMC+ or PMC3 lump clay
- PMC+ or PMC3 syringe clay
- 5×7mm fine-silver prong setting
- 5×7mm kiln-safe cubic zirconia (CZ)
- Badger Balm or olive oil
- plastic mat
- roller
- **22** playing cards
- unmounted stamp (regular thickness, not extra-heavy)
- cooking spray
- paper towel
- tweezers
- craft knife or scalpel
- cocktail straw
- metal file or emery board
- needle stylus (optional)
- small brush
- water
- steel brush
- burnisher
- tumbler (optional)
- liver of sulfur (optional)
- prong-setting pliers

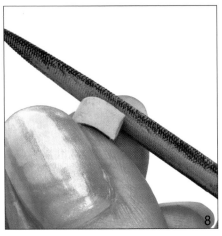

6 To make the bail, grease the cocktail straw and wrap the saved strip of clay around it. Join the ends together with syringe clay **[6]**. Let the clay impression and bail dry.

7-8 After the pieces have dried, remove the straw and file the edges of the pendant **[7]** and the bail **[8]**, making sure there are no sharp edges. Remove any filings from the bail. If you would like to sign the back of your piece, do so now using a needle stylus.

9 To attach the bail, use a brush to apply water to the pendant and the bail where they will connect. Place the bail in the desired spot **[9]** and secure them together with syringe clay. Let the piece dry. Check the bail and do touch-up filing if necessary. If any cracks appear, add more syringe clay, smooth, and let dry again. Fire according to the manufacturer's instructions.

10-11 Scrub the piece with a steel brush and then use the burnisher to bring out the highlights in the imprinted image **[10-11]**. If you have a tumbler, you can use that instead.

12 Use liver of sulfur to add a patina **[12]** if desired, as described on page 19.

13-15 Use the prong-setting pliers to set the CZ as described below.

described on page 19.

tip

Using prong-setting pliers

These specialized pliers are used to set stones and cubic zirconias (CZs) into a commercial prong setting. Hold the pliers in such a way that the groove straddles one of the prongs while the dimple in the pliers goes to the opposite prong. With the dimple part of the pliers, grab onto the prong and gently squeeze. The prong should move slightly. Change the position of the pliers so that the groove straddles the opposite prong (the prong that was just moved by the dimple part of the pliers); again, gently squeeze. Repeat this process with the opposite pair of prongs. Check if the stone is secure; if not, repeat the process.

11

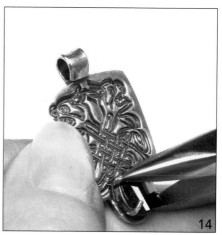

12

13

14

15

Textured link bracelet

Texture metal clay with lace and embellish it with cubic zirconias and syringe clay to create bracelet links. If you enjoy this technique, turn to page 45 for additional project ideas.

This textured bracelet offers a wonderful opportunity to play with color. Use lace to texture rolled-out clay, punch out geometric shapes with a clay cutter, and embellish each link with a different-colored cubic zirconia (CZ). Connect the links with wrapped loops and bicone crystals in a variety of colors. If you wish, experiment with larger, asymmetrical CZs or different textures.

1 Grease your plastic mat and roller, then roll the clay out to a thickness of three cards [1].

2-3 Add texture by placing the lace on top of the clay (without removing the cards) and rolling the clay again [2]. Remove the lace and make sure you have made a clear impression [3].

4-5 Using the clay cutter, punch out the shapes, getting the most shapes out of your piece of clay [4]. Remove the excess clay [5].

6 Using an ungreased cocktail straw, punch a hole in each of the shapes where you want a cubic zirconia (CZ) to rest [6]. As you punch the hole, the straw should pull out the clay. If the straw does not pull out the clay, take your tweezers and carefully pull out the bit of clay. Be certain not to punch the hole too close to the edge. Leave a margin of at least 3mm between the edge of the clay and the hole.

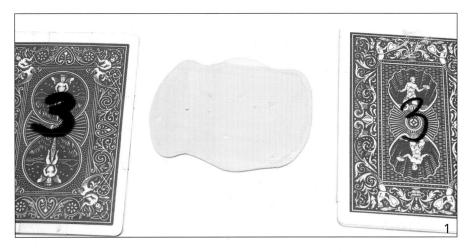

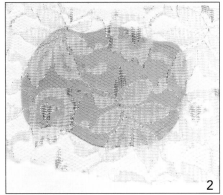

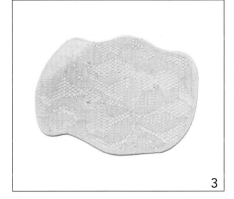

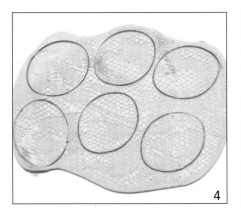

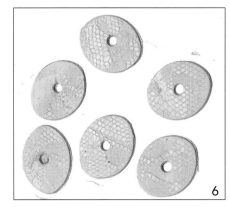

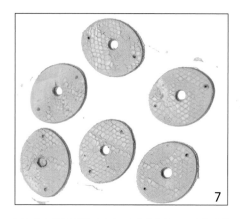

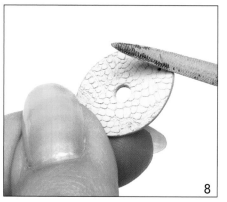

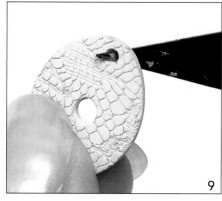

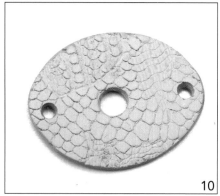

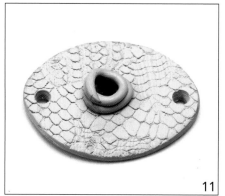

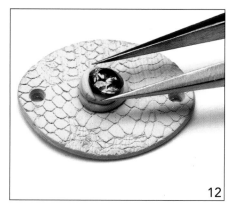

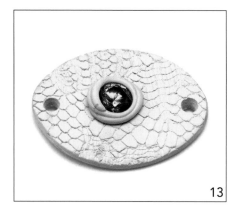

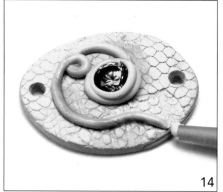

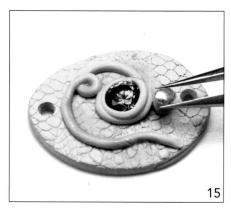

7 With your needle stylus, make a mark at two opposite ends of each shape **[7]**. These marks will become holes, which will be used for connecting the links together later. Mark the spots approximately 3mm from the edge. Do not create the holes at this stage; only mark the spots. Let each piece dry.

8 When all shapes are dry, file the edges with a metal file or emery board until they are smooth **[8]**.

9-10 To turn the marks made by the needle stylus in step 7 into holes, insert the tip of the craft knife carefully into each hole. Hold it at a right angle to the piece and rotate the knife without applying pressure. Turn the piece over and repeat so that the holes are even on both sides **[9]**. Repeat for the other hole on the piece **[10]**; then repeat the step for all the pieces. If you wish, sign one piece with a needle stylus.

11-13 Using a clean brush, create a wet trail around the hole created to set the CZ. Take the syringe clay and apply pressure to make a 5–10mm tail. Create a two- to three-tiered syringe-clay well around the hole **[11]**. Place your brush in the opening of the well, pushing out the walls of the well by gently moving the brush in a circular motion. If necessary, the outer walls of the well can be pushed in gently. Pick up the CZ with your tweezers and place it on top of the still-wet well **[12]**. Gently push the CZ in with

17

18

19

tip

A Note on Wire

You can use almost any wire to make the wrapped-loop connectors for this bracelet. Gold-filled or fine silver are the most expensive options, while sterling silver makes a practical alternative because it's harder than fine silver and therefore will wear better. For best results, use half-hard wire.

your tweezers. The edge of the well should be above the edge of the CZ [13]. If it isn't, make a wet trail with your brush and then add a string of syringe clay across the surface of the CZ; this will help keep the CZ secure after firing. Repeat, adding a CZ to each piece in the same manner.

14 To embellish your pieces and to place the stringer over the CZ, always make a wet trail with your brush first and then add a syringe-clay tail [14]. You can create many different patterns, such as spirals, lines, and zigzags. Add as much or as little as you want. Remember to take your wet brush and gently touch your newly added syringe clay with the side of the brush to help it attach to the rest of the piece.

15-16 Determine where you wish to add casting grain. Wet the desired spots with a brush, place your syringe above the area, and squeeze out a blob of clay approximately the same size as the casting grain. Pick up the casting grain with tweezers and place it on top of the syringe-clay blob [15]. Use the end of the tweezers to gently push the casting grain all the way into the blob, which will create a bezel (or setting) for the grain [16]. Dry the pieces and fire according to the manufacturer's instructions.

17-18 Scrub the piece with a steel brush and burnish it until the silver shines [17]. If you have a tumbler, you can use that instead. If you wish, use liver of sulfur to add a patina [18] as described on page 19.

19 Cut a 3-in. [7.62cm] piece of wire and make the first half of a wrapped loop (see pages 20-21 for wireworking instructions.) Slide one of the metal links onto the loop and complete the loop. String a 4mm bicone crystal on the wire, make the first half of a wrapped loop, and slide on another metal link. Finish the wrapped loop. Continue linking the textured components with crystal links and attach half of the

clasp after the last crystal link at each end [19].

materials

- PMC+ lump clay
- PMC+ syringe clay
- casting grain
- kiln-safe cubic zirconias (CZs)
- 4mm bicone crystals
- toggle clasp
- wire
- Badger Balm or olive oil
- plastic mat
- roller
- **6** playing cards
- lace
- clay cutter
- cocktail straw
- tweezers
- needle stylus
- metal file or emery board
- craft knife
- small brush
- water
- steel brush
- burnisher
- tumbler (optional)
- liver of sulfur (optional)
- chainnose pliers
- roundnose pliers
- wire cutters

Leaf imprint pendant and earrings

Combine two natural elements—leaves and pearls—for a memorable pendant-and-earring set. If you enjoy this technique, turn to page 46 for additional project ideas.

Leaves and trees are very inspiring to me, and I love finding ways to use them in my designs. This simple pendant-and-earring set is one of my favorites, and I make different versions when I find new leaves that I like.

You can use cubic zirconias to embellish your metal clay leaves if you wish, but I like to add pearls to mine, letting a natural material complement a natural texture.

Pendant

1 Grease your plastic mat and roller, then roll the clay out to a thickness of four cards **[1]**. Be sure to roll out an area large enough so that it will accommodate the leaf, leaving an additional 15mm of clay where the bail will be located.

2-3 Remove the stem of the leaf. Place the leaf on the clay, vein side down, and roll over it to make an imprint in the clay, making sure that your roller rests on the card stacks at all times **[2]**. Carefully remove the leaf, using tweezers if necessary **[3]**.

4-5 Using a craft knife or scalpel, trim the excess clay around the leaf image, leaving a 1–2mm margin if desired **[4]**. Leave a tapered wedge at least 15mm long for the bail **[5]**.

6-7 To make the bail, liberally grease the cocktail straw.

1

2

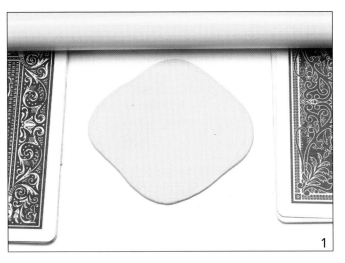

3

4

5

6

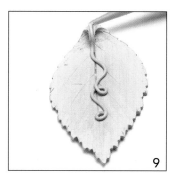

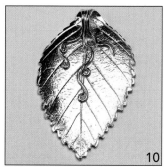

Place the straw at the base of the wedge that is intended for the bail [6]. Roll the tail of the wedge over the straw and put a drop of syringe clay on the underside of the tip of the wedge to adhere the clay where it touches [7]. Use a ball stylus to gently press the tip of the bail into place; do not use your fingertip to press as it will leave an imprint. Let the piece dry.

8 Once the piece has dried, use a metal file or an emery board to smooth the edges of the pendant and bail so there are no sharp edges [8]. If you are planning on signing your piece, do so now with a needle stylus.

9 To embellish the leaf, use a wet brush to make a trail and then add a syringe-clay tail to create spirals or other organic designs [9]. Do not add much syringe clay to the bail because you will be adding a pearl later. Remember to take your wet brush and gently touch your newly added embellishment with the side of the brush in order to help the clay attach to the rest of the piece. Let the piece dry and fire it according to the manufacturer's instructions.

10 Scrub the piece with a brass brush and polish it with a burnisher until the silver shines [10]. If you have a tumbler, you can use that instead. If you wish, use liver of sulfur to add a patina as described on page 19.

11 String a pearl onto a headpin and make the first half of a wrapped loop (see pages 20-21 for wireworking instructions). Slide the loop onto the bail and complete the loop [11].

Earrings

12-16 Grease your plastic mat and roller, then roll the clay out to a thickness of four cards [12]. Remove the stem of the smaller leaf. Place the leaf on the clay, vein side down, and roll over it to make an imprint in the clay, making sure that your roller rests on the card stacks at all times [13]. Remove the leaf, carefully, using tweezers if necessary [14]. Move the leaf over for the second earring and roll over it again to imprint it into the clay, taking care not to mar the first imprint [15]. Remove the leaf and check to make sure that the two imprints are clear [16].

17-18 Trim the excess clay around the leaf imprints, leave a 1–2mm margin around the image if desired [17].

materials

- PMC+ or PMC3 lump clay
- PMC+ or PMC3 syringe clay
- **3** pearls
- **3** 24-gauge sterling-silver headpins
- **2** French hook ear wires
- Badger Balm or olive oil
- plastic mat
- roller
- **8** playing cards
- **2** leaves: a larger one for the pendant, and a smaller, symmetrical leaf for the earrings (both leaves should have well-defined veins)
- tweezers
- craft knife or scalpel
- cocktail straw
- ball stylus
- metal file or emery board
- needle stylus (optional)
- small brush
- water
- steel brush
- burnisher
- tumbler (optional)
- liver of sulfur (optional)
- roundnose pliers
- chainnose pliers
- wire cutters

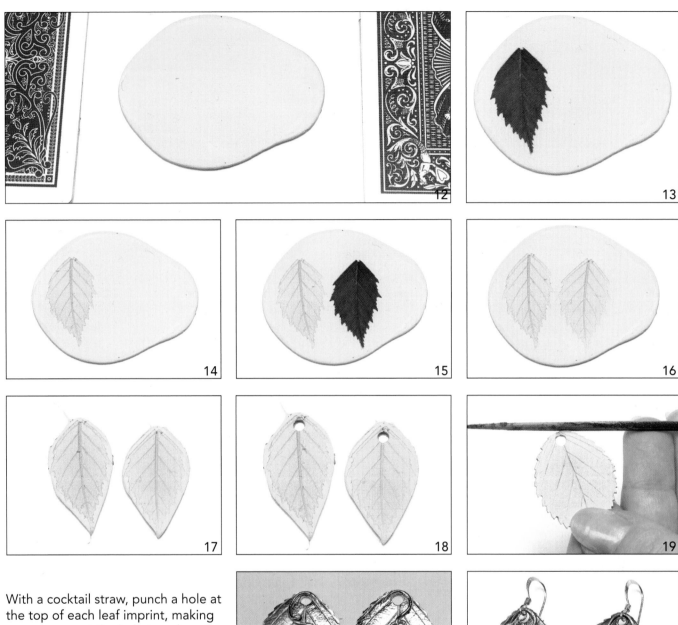

With a cocktail straw, punch a hole at the top of each leaf imprint, making sure not to put the hole too close to the edge [18]. Leave approximately 3mm between the hole and the top of the leaf. Let the pieces dry.

19 Use a metal file or an emery board to smooth the edges of each earring component so there are no sharp edges [19]. Be very careful not to file too much away from the edge above the hole. If you are planning on signing your pieces, do so now with a needle stylus. If desired, embellish the earring pieces by adding small spirals or other organic elements with syringe clay, as described in step 9.

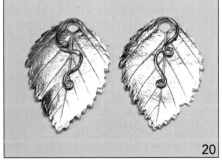

20 Dry the pieces and fire them according to the manufacturer's instructions. Scrub the pieces with a steel brush and polish them with a burnisher until the silver shines [20]. If you have a tumbler, you can use that instead. If you wish, use liver of sulfur to add a patina, as described on page 19.

21 Open the loop (see pages 20-21) on an ear wire. Slide the loop through the hole in one of the earring leaves. Close the loop. String a pearl onto a headpin and make the first half of a wrapped loop. Slide the loop onto the ear wire in front of the leaf. Complete the loop and attach it to the ear wire in front of the leaf component with a wrapped loop. Repeat with the other earring. [21].

Use metal clay scraps and 2-4mm beads from your stash to create this gem-wrapped bead. If you enjoy this technique, turn to page 47 for additional project ideas.

All beaders have stashes of beads left over from other projects—a few sparkling crystals here, a few smooth pearls there. And metal clay artisans have stashes too—small clay scraps left over from larger pieces. Making this bead is a great way to use both of your stashes. Use lump clay for the base, and embellish the ends with a little syringe clay; then string your bead stash on wire and wrap it around the fired silver bead.

1 Grease your plastic mat and roller, then roll the clay out to a thickness of three cards. If you use a cocktail straw for this project, cut out a piece of clay approximately 7×15mm in size; if you use a drinking straw, cut the clay 10×20mm or larger, depending on the size of the straw.

2-3 Wrap the clay around the chosen straw and use syringe clay to "glue" the seam [2].

Smooth the seam with a blending tool so that it becomes invisible [3].

4-5 Remove the tip of the syringe applicator so that it will produce a larger coil. Begin to build the end caps of the bead, starting at the edge. Make four to five coils of syringe [4] and compress them with a very wet brush to ensure that there are no gaps [5]. Repeat for the other end cap.

6-7 Replace the syringe tip and determine where you wish to add casting grain. Wet the desired spot with a brush, place your syringe over the area, and squeeze out a blob of clay approximately the same size as the casting grain [6]. Pick up the casting grain with tweezers and place it on top of the blob. Use the end of the tweezers to gently push the casting grain all the way into the blob, which will create a setting for the grain [7, page 42].

1

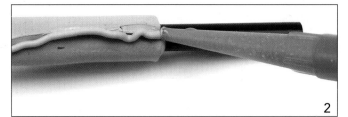
2

3

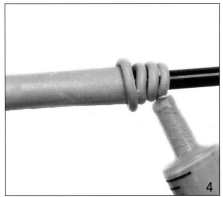
4

5

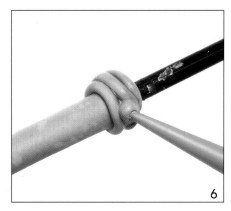
6

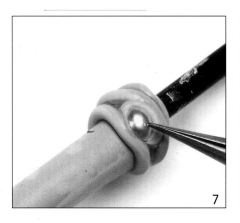

7

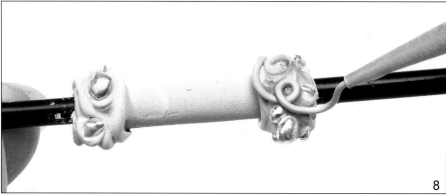

8

9

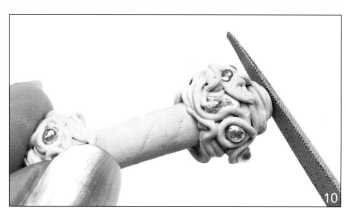

10

11

12

materials

- PMC+ or PMC3 lump clay
- PMC+ or PMC3 syringe clay
- casting grain
- 12–18 in. [30.48-45.72cm] of 24-gauge sterling silver wire
- assorted 2–4mm gemstone beads and pearls
- Badger Balm or olive oil
- plastic mat
- roller
- **6** playing cards
- craft knife or scalpel
- straw
- blender
- tweezers
- metal file or emery board
- steel brush
- burnisher
- tumbler (optional)

8-9 Add several more coils of syringe clay at each end cap for a tapered look. Embellish with more syringe clay, making a pleasing pattern of coils and lines **[8-9]**. Let the bead dry.

10 Once the bead is dry, file the edges to remove any sharp points **[10]**. Fire the piece according to the manufacturer's instructions.

11 Scrub the piece with a steel brush and polish it with a burnisher until the silver shines **[11]**. If you have a tumbler, you can use that instead.

tip

If you'd like to make a bead with a smaller hole, use a toothpick as the base. You don't need to grease the toothpick or remove it before firing; it will burn out in the kiln.

12 String assorted pearls and gemstones on the sterling-silver wire and wrap the beaded wire around the center of the silver bead, filling the space between the end

caps. When the space is filled, wrap the ends around one of the wire coils and tuck them underneath the wired-on beads **[12]**.

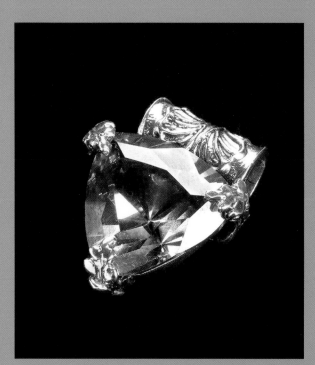

Use a stamp to decorate a bail.

Use a stamp to imprint a ring.

You can use fully or partially stamped images to create bracelet and earring components. Use the same stamp to make the bracelet's clasp.

GALLERY

Create a three-strand Celtic centerpiece by stacking two layers of clay with three parallel pieces of wire in between. Remove the wire before firing.

Make Celtic earring links by creating holes in the top and bottom of each component. Attach an earring wire in the top hole, and wrapped-loop dangles from the bottom hole.

Make multiple components with the same design to create matching necklace-and-earring sets.

Experiment with different textures for bracelet links. Stamps, leaves, and texture plates work well. The components of this heart set were textured with a stamp.

Vary the bracelet design by using different shapes and sizes of clay cutters.

Use larger, irregularly shaped cubic zirconias for more color and a three-dimensional effect.

Make multiple holes on the sides of each leaf and use them in a multistrand necklace. A hole at the tip of a leaf can accommodate a dangle.

Right: Use graduated leaves in different shapes to create bracelet components.

Make a variety of earrings, rings, and pendants using different leaves. If you wish, trim the imprinted clay into a non-leaf shape, as with the heart-shaped earrings here. Use cubic zirconias in combination with the leaf textures.

Create this leaf-imprinted bracelet on a curved mandrel.

Use your gem-wrapped bead as a centerpiece for a multistrand necklace, using the rest of the beads from your stash to complement it!

Make earrings & a cuff bracelet with fine silver wire. Instead of building the piece around a straw, construct it around a piece of wire (16-gauge or heavier). You can coat the wire with a heavy layer of paste for more strength. To make the cuff, curve the wire first.

Intermediate
Projects

In this chapter, you'll explore nine projects that build on some of the techniques learned in the previous chapter. These projects will also introduce you to some more advanced techniques. They're a bit more complicated, but mastery of the techniques and materials presented in this chapter will prepare you for making your own fabulous creations.

Create a smooth, seamless bead by painting layers of metal clay paste over a cork clay base. If you enjoy this technique, turn to page 86 for additional project ideas.

After rolling, cutting, and trimming metal clay, it can be very soothing and relaxing to make a cork clay base and slowly coat it with metal clay paste. This creates a smooth, seamless, three-dimensional bead that's very rewarding to decorate.

I also use the process described below to make vessels based on ancient shapes. To see some examples of vessels, turn to page 86.

1–2 Cut a piece of cork clay and mold it into the shape that you want the bead to be—typically an oval **[1]** or a round shape. Use the end of the skewer to pierce the cork clay in the location where you want the hole to be, and leave the cork bead on the end of the skewer **[2]**. Let the cork dry.

3–4 Once the cork is dry, use a brush to coat it with paste **[3]**. Let the first coat dry and apply a second. Repeat until you have applied 6–10 coats of paste (you'll notice that the piece feels heavier after a few coats). Make sure to let each coat dry completely before applying the next one. The first coats will dry quickly, but the subsequent coats will require ever-longer drying times. Be patient! If you rush the process and add a coat when the previous coat is not yet fully dry, you may rehydrate the underlying coats, which will cause them to stick to your brush and peel off. Let the piece dry after applying the last coat **[4]**.

5 Once the piece has dried, use a metal file around the edges to carefully remove excess dried paste **[5]**. Don't worry about damaging the skewer; it is more important to file the excess paste around the holes. If you would like to even out the paste on the bead itself, use sandpaper, an emery board, or a sanding pad with a fine grit. Take care not to apply too

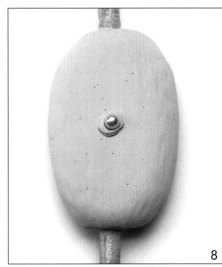

much pressure or you could crack the metal-clay paste veneer over the cork clay.

6–14 Embellish your bead using casting grain, cubic zirconias (CZs), or syringe clay—or all three!

To set the casting grain, wet the spot where you want to apply the grain. Squeeze out a blob of syringe clay approximately the same size as the grain that you are about to set **[6]**. Use tweezers to pick up the casting grain and place it on top of the syringe-clay blob **[7]**; gently push the grain all the way into the blob **[8]**.

To set a 2mm CZ, repeat the technique used to attach the casting grain, but make sure that the edges of the CZ sink slightly below the surface of the syringe clay **[9]**. To set a 3mm or larger CZ, use the syringe clay to create a well large enough to accommodate the CZ **[10]**. Set the CZ in the well and make certain that its edges sink below the top tier of the well **[11]**. If you are not certain whether the CZ's edges are sunk low enough, then secure the CZ with a stringer or tail of syringe clay.

To embellish with syringe clay, make sure to wet the bead first, and then take an organic, freeform approach to extruding syringe clay on the bead **[12]**.

Continue to embellish all sides of the bead with syringe clay, casting grain, and CZs **[13–14]**. When you have a design you like, make sure to use a damp brush to properly adhere the syringe clay to the bead's surface. Let the piece dry .

15–16 Once the piece has dried, cut off or break the skewer, leaving ½–1 in. [1.27-2.54cm] protruding from the bead. Be careful not to damage the piece while removing the skewer. Fire the piece according to the manufacturer's instructions.

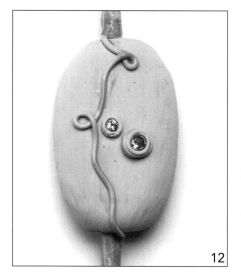

12

13

14

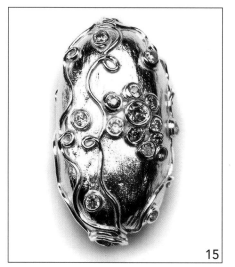

15

16

17

Scrub the piece with a steel brush and polish it with a burnisher until the silver shines **[15]**. If you have a tumbler, you can use that instead. If you wish, use liver of sulfur to add a patina **[16]** as described on page 19.

Vessel

To make a vessel, cut a piece of cork clay and mold it into the shape that you want the vessel to be. Use the end of the skewer to pierce the vessel in the location where you want the hole to be, making certain that the skewer does not go all the way through the vessel. Leave the cork vessel on the end of the skewer **[17]**. Follow steps 2–16 above to finish the vessel.

materials

- PMC+ or PMC3 paste
- PMC+ or PMC3 syringe clay
- assorted kiln-safe cubic zirconias (CZs) (optional)
- casting grain (optional)
- cork clay
- wooden skewer
- small brush
- metal file
- fine-grit sandpaper, emery board, or sanding pad
- tweezers
- water
- steel brush
- burnisher
- tumbler (optional)
- liver of sulfur (optional)

Seedpod pendant

Cover both sides of a deep seedpod with metal clay paste. Decorate the pod with syringe and add a cubic zirconia. If you enjoy this technique, turn to pages 87–88 for additional project ideas.

Seedpod pendants (and earrings, too) are my all-time favorite projects to make! I've been collecting seedpods longer than I've been making jewelry. Whenever I travel, I collect seedpods from different climates and regions as mementos of special trips. Metal clay allows me to transform my mementos into jewelry that will last forever.

I love to experiment with combining two (or more) types of pods, as you can see on page 88. If you're feeling adventurous, you can do the same!

1

2

3

4

5

6

7

8

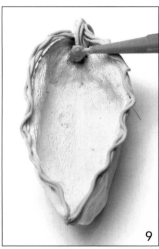

9

materials

- PMC+ or PMC3 paste
- PMC+ or PMC3 syringe clay
- seedpod (deep, with an unusual or interesting texture)
- assorted CZs
- food dehydrator (optional)
- small brush
- Badger Balm or olive oil
- cocktail straw
- tweezers
- water
- metal file or emery board
- steel brush
- burnisher
- tumbler (optional)
- liver of sulfur (optional)

1 Choose a seedpod to use. The best pods are relatively deep and have an interesting texture on the outside **[1]**. The pod you use must be thoroughly dry; if you're not certain it's dry or you want to dry out a newly picked seedpod, place the pod in a food dehydrator. Make certain to designate or create a spot for the bail.

2 Apply the first coat of paste to the pod **[2]** and let dry. Once the first coat is dry, apply a second coat. Repeat until 6–10 coats have been applied, making sure that each coat has dried completely before applying the next one. Once the last coat of paste has been applied, let your piece dry thoroughly.

3 Embellish the pod as desired with syringe clay **[3]**. Let the piece dry and fire it according to the manufacturer's instructions.

4 To create the bail, grease a cocktail straw and wrap a syringe-clay tail several times around the straw until you have reached the desired width **[4]**. Let the bail dry.

5–8 Use syringe clay to attach the bail to the rest of the piece, wetting both the bail and the piece first **[5–6]**. Embellish with syringe clay over the bail, continuing onto the rest of the piece, both front and back, to integrate the bail into the design **[7]**. Continue syringe clay work onto the edges of the pod to cover any rough spots **[8]**.

9–14 Choose a spot to set a cubic zirconia (CZ). If your CZ is 2–3mm, squeeze out a blob of syringe clay approximately the same size as the CZ **[9]**. Pick up the CZ with your tweezers, place it on top of the blob, and gently push it all the way into the blob **[10]**. Be

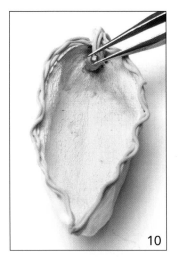

10

11

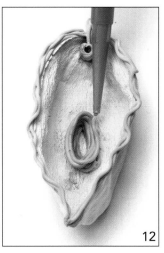

12

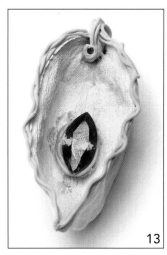

13

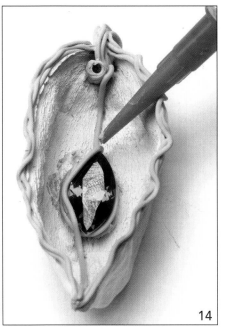

14

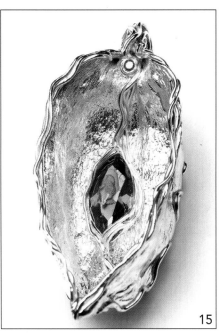

15

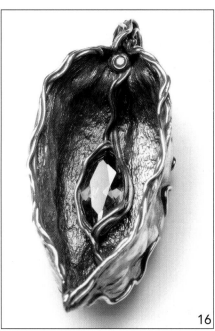

16

certain that the edges of the CZ sink slightly below the surface of the blob **[11]**.

If your CZ is 4mm or larger, create a well large enough to accommodate it **[12]**, place the CZ in the well **[13]**, and make certain that the edges of the CZ sink below the top tier of the well. If you aren't certain that the edges are secure enough, then add a stringer or tail of syringe clay **[14]**. Use this same reinforcing technique for any non-round CZ you add.

15–16 Dry the completed piece and file any rough spots with a metal file or an emery board. Fire according to the manufacturer's instructions. Scrub the piece with a steel brush and polish it with a burnisher until the silver shines **[15]**. If you have a tumbler, you can use that instead. If you wish, use liver of sulfur to add a patina **[16]** as described on page 19.

tip

Watching paste dry

Waiting for each coat of paste to dry thoroughly before applying the next coat can be time-consuming. Speed up the drying process by using a hair dryer. You can also place the piece in a food dehydrator.

Fold, cut, and glue metal clay sheet to make a lovely kimono-shaped pendant. If you enjoy this technique, turn to page 89 for additional project ideas.

I've always been fascinated by Japanese art and culture, and I've found the clean, elegant lines of traditional kimonos particularly appealing. Origami, the art of paper folding, has also intrigued me. Here, I combined my two interests by folding metal clay sheet to create this kimono-shaped pendant.

This pendant uses a minimal amount of syringe, but you can add more if you wish (see page 89 for an example). Make sure to use water sparingly, so the sheet clay does not disintegrate.

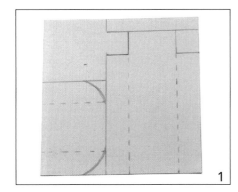

1

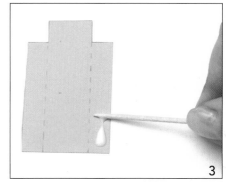

2

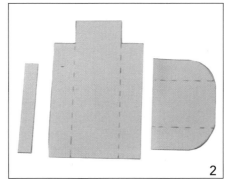

3

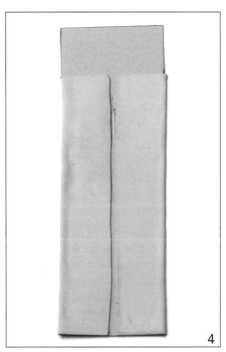

4

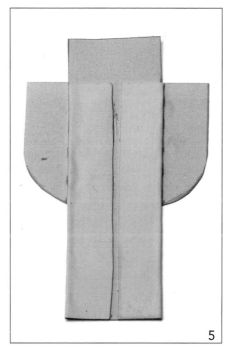

5

1 With pencil and ruler, lightly draw the kimono pattern from page 61 directly onto the PMC+ sheet [1], being very careful to not press the pencil into the sheet hard enough to score the surface.

2 Using sharp scissors, cut along the outlines of the pieces (the solid lines in the kimono pattern) [2]. Do not cut along the dotted lines.

3–4 Take Part A (the central piece) and fold the sides in along the dotted lines. Use your fingers to make a crease. Once you are certain that both folds are straight, open the folds flat again and apply Elmer's glue onto the insides of the folds, using a toothpick to spread the glue evenly [3]. Press the folds down closed again [4].

5 Take Part B (the curved piece) and apply glue to the center portion between the dotted lines.

Carefully place Part A, with the folded sides up, onto Part B, positioned as shown in [5].

6–7 Turn the piece over. Place a toothpick just above

Part B [6, page 60]. Apply glue to the tab at the top of Part A. Roll the tab tightly over the toothpick so that it overlaps onto Part B and glue it in place [7, page 60].

6

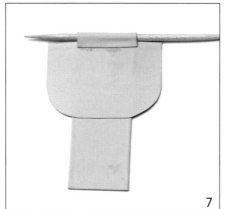

7

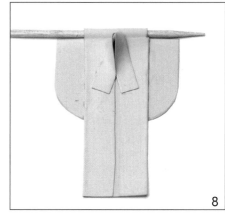

8

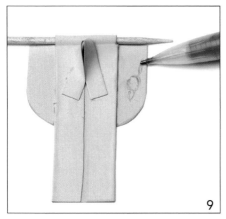

9

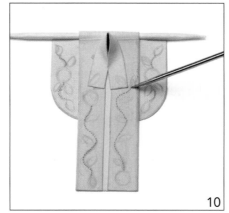

10

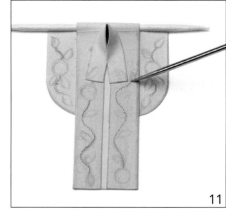

11

12

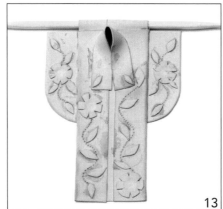

13

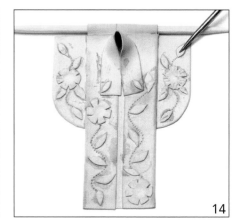

14

8 Turn the piece right side up. Take Part C (the rectangular strip), fold it in half, and position it on Part A. This is the collar to the kimono and can be arranged as you see fit. Once you are satisfied with the placement, lightly mark the spot with a pencil. Apply glue to the ends of Part C and place it carefully onto the piece, making sure the ends are even **[8]**.

9–10 Lightly draw a design onto the kimono with a pencil **[9–10]**.

11 Take the needle stylus and lightly score the lines that you want to look stitched **[11]**.

12 To make flowers to ornament the kimono, cut out four small circles, approximately 5–6mm in diameter, from your remaining pieces of sheet clay. You can use scrapbooking paper punches if you have the right size. Cut six tiny wedge shapes from the edge of each circle. Cut out leaf shapes as well; these can vary in size but should be about 2×5mm each **[12]**.

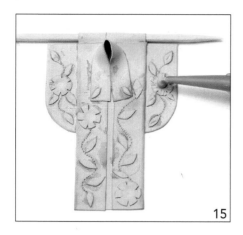

15

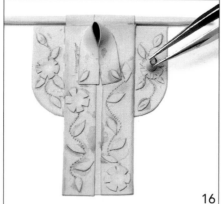

16

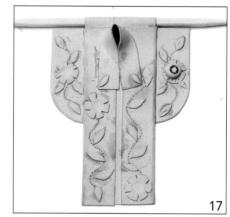

17

18

19

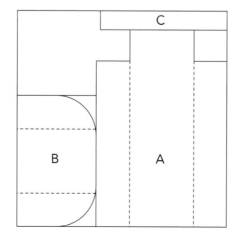

20

13 Take all of the components from step 12 and glue them onto the front of the kimono [13].

14 To texture the leaves and flowers, use the needle stylus to lightly score each leaf, creating veins, and make tiny imprints on the flower petals in between the cut-out wedges [14].

15–17 To set the cubic zirconias (CZs), take the ball stylus and imprint it into the center of each flower, making an indentation. Make a blob with your syringe clay approximately the size of the CZ [15]. Use the tweezers to set the CZ on top of the blob and carefully push it in [16], making sure that the edge of the CZ is submerged. Continue, adding the desired number of CZs [17].

18–20 Leave the toothpick in place [18] and fire according to the manufacturer's instructions. The toothpick will burn away in the kiln and create a bail for a slender chain or rope. Scrub the piece with a steel brush and polish it with a burnisher until the silver shines [19]. If you have a tumbler, you can use that instead. If you wish, use liver of sulfur to add a patina [20] as described on page 19.

materials

- PMC+ sheet clay
- PMC+ or PMC3 syringe clay
- 4mm kiln-safe CZs
- pencil
- sharp scissors
- Elmer's glue
- toothpicks
- pencil
- needle stylus
- scrapbooking paper punches (optional)
- ball stylus
- tweezers
- steel brush
- burnisher
- tumbler (optional)
- liver of sulfur (optional)

Set a brilliant, reflective dichoric cabochon in a simple frame of PMC3 syringe clay. If you enjoy this technique, turn to page 90 for additional project ideas.

I enjoy using colorful, reflective dichroic glass in my jewelry. The many colors that make up each piece remind me of natural opals, which are far too delicate to be fired with metal clay. However, with the introduction of PMC3 and its lower firing temperature, it's easy to incorporate dichroic glass into metal clay pieces.

I chose syringe clay to set the cabochon for this pendant. It makes a smooth setting, and the simple syringe frame doesn't obscure the glass, allowing the cabochon to be the focal point.

1

2

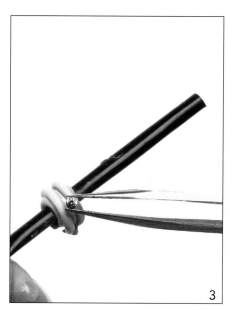
3

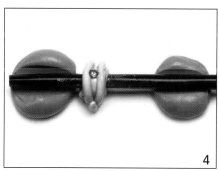
4

1–2 Grease the cocktail straw. Remove the cap from the syringe and do not put on the tip. Wind a syringe-clay trail around the straw multiple times. (It's all right if the syringe clay breaks in the process; just continue winding around.) Create two or three layers to give the bail a chunky, organic look [1]. With a very wet brush, pat the syringe clay down until there are no gaps in the bail [2].

3 With your tweezers, set a cubic zirconia (CZ) in the front of the bail [3]. Push it in until the edge of the CZ is slightly below the level of the syringe-clay bail.

4 Place the bail on the straw rests and let it dry thoroughly [4].

5

6

7

materials

- PMC3 syringe clay
- 2mm kiln-safe cubic zirconia (CZ)
- 15–25mm dichroic glass cabochon
- 4mm sterling-silver split ring
- 1 in. [2.54cm] sterling-silver chain with large links
- **15–20** round 2mm sterling-silver beads
- assorted 6mm Swarovski crystals
- **15–20** 24-gauge sterling-silver headpins
- Badger Balm or olive oil
- cocktail straw
- small brush
- water
- tweezers
- **2** straw rests
- plastic mat
- metal file
- sanding pads
- craft knife or scalpel
- steel brush
- burnisher
- tumbler (optional)
- chainnose pliers
- roundnose pliers
- wire cutters (preferably flush)
- split-ring pliers

8

9

5–7 Place your dichroic glass cabochon on the plastic mat **[5]** and decide where you wish to place the bail. With your syringe clay, make a loop around the entire cabochon, creating a gap between the syringe clay and the cabochon opposite from where the bail will be **[6]**. Make several additional loops with the syringe clay around the edge of the cabochon. On your last pass, drape a syringe-clay tail across the front of the cabochon to secure it **[7]**.

8 With a very wet brush, shape the end of the tail to taper

and smooth it into the rest of the syringe-clay bezel **[8]**. Pat the rest of the bezel down with your brush to make sure there are no gaps between the cabochon and the bezel. If necessary, shape the bezel and the loop below it. Avoid touching the top surface of the glass cabochon with the brush if at all possible, as the metal clay can leave a film on the glass after firing.

9 Remove the dry bail from the straw and push it into the wet bezel in the desired location. With your brush, shape any section of the bezel that might become distorted

10

11

12

13

14

tip

For a slightly different look—but still plenty of sparkle—make this project with a large, kiln-safe cubic zirconia (CZ) instead of a dichroic cabochon.

13 Fire the piece according to the manufacturer's instructions. Scrub the piece with a steel brush (be careful not to scratch the glass) and polish it with a burnisher until the silver shines **[13]**. If you have a tumbler, you can use that instead.

14 Attach the split ring (see pages 20-21) to the loop at the bottom of the piece and attach the chain to the split ring. String a silver bead and a crystal on a head pin. Make the first half of a wrapped loop (see pages 20-21) and slide the loop onto the first link of the chain. Complete the loop. Repeat, adding 10–14 beaded head pins to the chain. Make five more beaded head pins, adding two to the left of the split ring and three to the right of the split ring **[14]**.

in the process of attaching the bail **[9]**. If necessary, reinforce with more syringe clay where the bail meets the bezel, but make sure not to close the hole in the bail. Let the piece dry.

10 Use a metal file and sanding pads to smooth the bezel and bail so that there are no sharp edges **[10]**. Turn your piece over and check the syringe-clay work. Put the tip on your syringe and fill any gaps; use a wet brush to push the syringe clay into spots that need to be filled. Dry the piece again and check a second time for any spots that need filing or filling.

11–12 Use a craft knife or scalpel to scrape off any residue on the surface of the cabochon **[11]**. Remove as much residue as possible to avoid developing a film on the glass after firing. Brush the cabochon clean with a dry brush **[12]**.

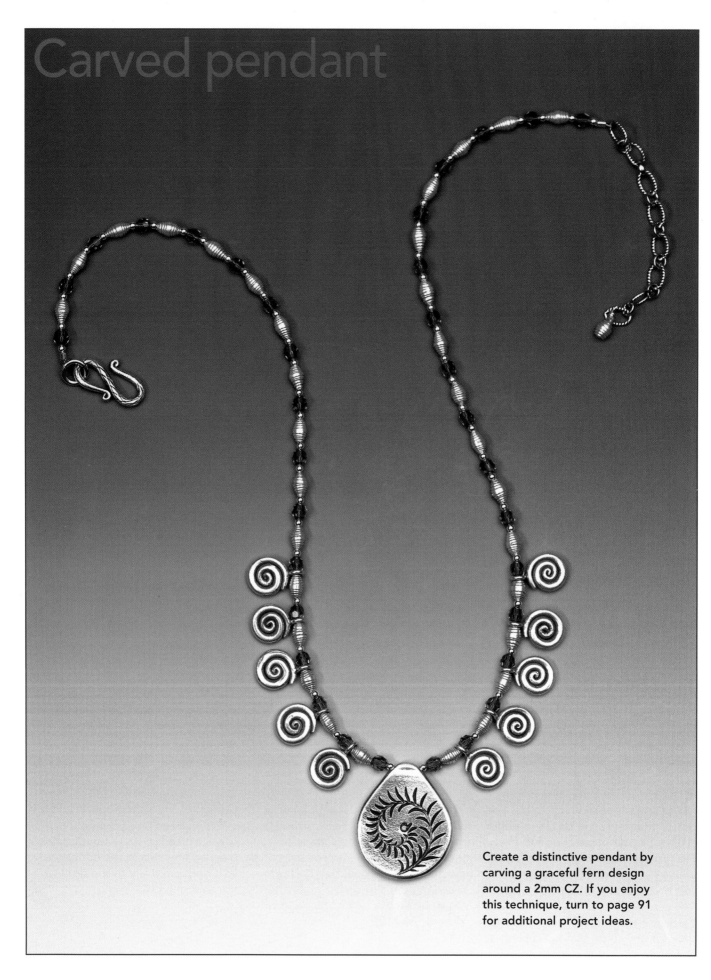

Create a distinctive pendant by carving a graceful fern design around a 2mm CZ. If you enjoy this technique, turn to page 91 for additional project ideas.

Though I work with stamps frequently, I also enjoy drawing unique designs by hand and then carving them into metal clay. Many of my carvings, including the one on this pendant, are inspired by the graceful lines of trees and ferns.

PMC Standard's shrinkage rate of 30% worked to my advantage in this project; I was able to plan and carve the design on a larger scale, allowing for greater detail.

1 Grease your plastic mat and roller, then roll the clay out to a thickness of six cards **[1]**.

2–3 Cut two identical shapes out of the clay using a craft knife, scalpel, or clay cutter **[2]**. Carefully remove the excess clay **[3]**.

4–5 Place a toothpick at the top of one of the shapes at least 5mm from the edge. Gently push the toothpick into the clay **[4]**. With a brush, wet the surface of the shape holding the toothpick. Wet one side of the other shape as well **[5]**. Put the second shape on top of the first shape, placing the wet sides together and covering the toothpick.

6 Add six more cards to each side (for a total of 12 cards on each side) and roll again to integrate the pieces **[6]**. Subtract one card on each side (for a total of 11 cards on each side) and roll once more to be certain the two pieces adhere to each other.

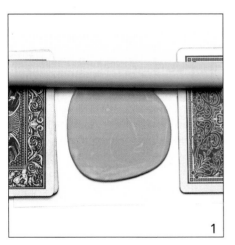

1

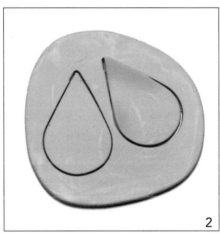

2

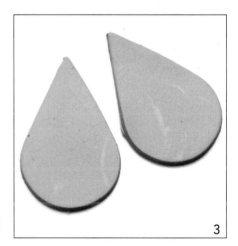

3

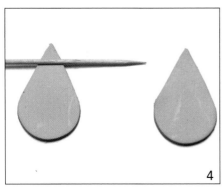

4

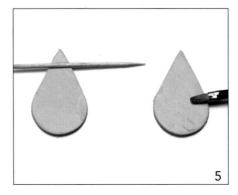

5

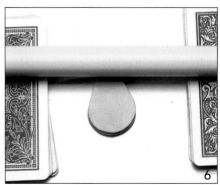

6

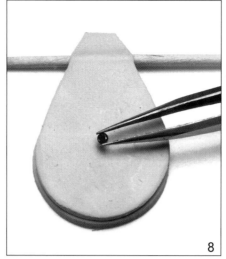

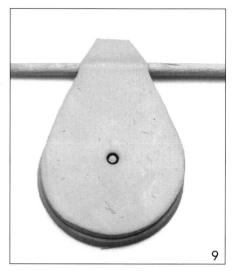

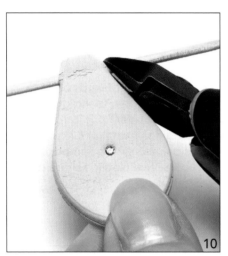

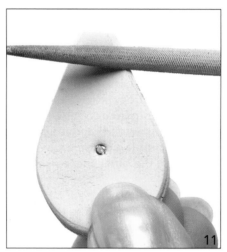

7 Using a craft knife or scalpel, trim off the point of the shape, making a straight line **[7]**.

8–9 Set the cubic zirconia (CZ) in the center of the piece with the tweezers **[8]**. Be sure that the edge of the CZ is below the line of the clay **[9]**. Let the piece dry.

10 Cut off the ends of the toothpick, getting as close to the sides of the pendant as you can **[10]**.

11–12 Use your metal file, emery board, and sanding pads to smooth the pendant's edges **[11]**. Be sure to file the areas around the toothpick at the same time to keep them even **[12]**. If you are planning on signing your piece, do so now using a needle stylus.

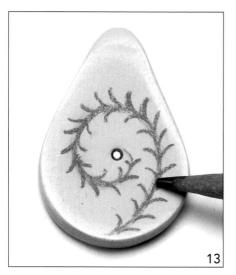

13

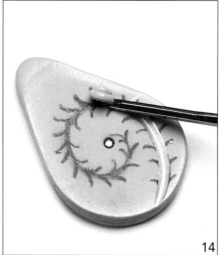

14

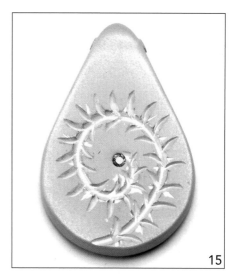

15

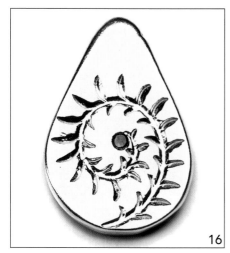

16

17

materials

- PMC Standard clay
- 2mm kiln-safe cubic zirconia (CZ)
- Badger Balm or olive oil
- plastic mat
- roller
- **24** playing cards
- craft knife or scalpel
- clay cutter (optional)
- toothpick
- small brush
- water
- tweezers
- wire cutters (preferably flush cutters)
- metal file or emery board
- sanding pads
- needle stylus (optional)
- pencil
- carving tools
- steel brush
- burnisher
- tumbler (optional)
- liver of sulfur (optional)

13 Use a pencil to lightly sketch your design on the surface of the dry piece [**13**].

14–15 Carve your design into the surface using the carving tools [**14**]. Follow the lines drawn in the previous step, using gentle, even pressure. Use a clean, dry brush to sweep away the debris from carving [**15**].

16–17 Fire the piece according to the manufacturer's instructions. Scrub the piece with a steel brush and polish it with a burnisher until the silver shines [**16**]. If you have a tumbler, you can use that instead. If you wish, use liver of sulfur to add a patina [**17**] as described on page 19.

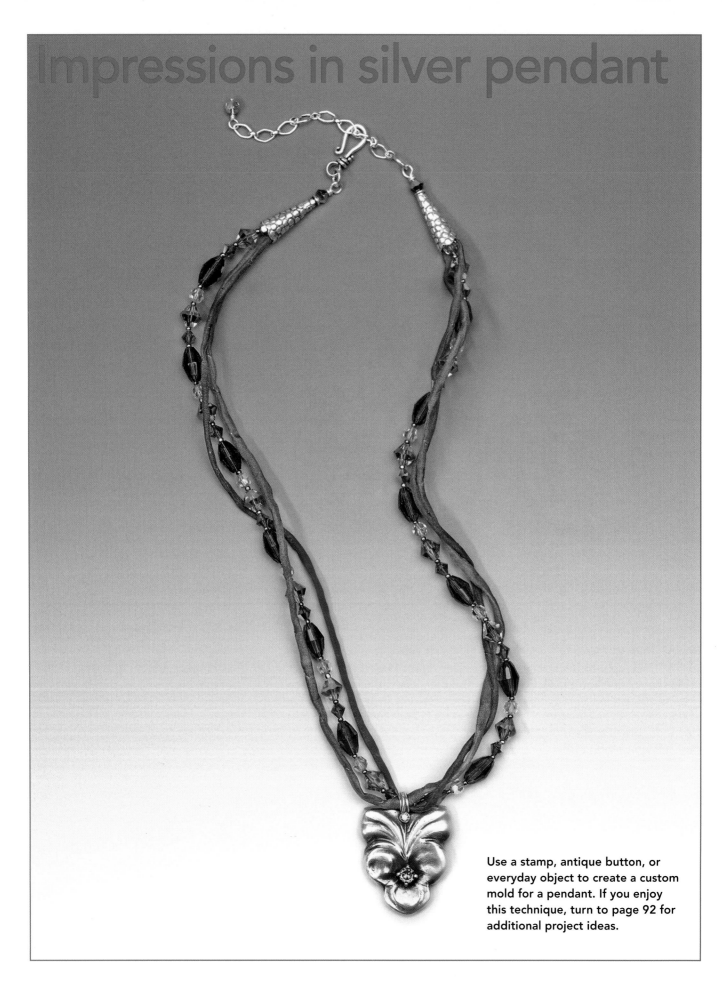

Use a stamp, antique button, or everyday object to create a custom mold for a pendant. If you enjoy this technique, turn to page 92 for additional project ideas.

In addition to seedpods, I also collect antique buttons, glass, and brass stampings, as well as fossils—anything with an interesting pattern or texture. I was delighted to discover that, with the use of two-part molding compound, I could create custom molds out of all of these objects and use them to make metal clay pieces.

You can also use stamps to create a mold, as I did with the project here.

1–2 Measure out equal parts of the two-part molding compound **[1]** and combine them. Knead them together long enough to make the color uniform **[2]**. Shape the compound to approximately the form of the object you are about to imprint. (For example, if you are making a mold of a round button, keep the putty round. If you are making a mold of an elongated object, roll out the material in a longer shape.) Take a flat object—an anvil works well—and flatten your piece of mold material against it until it is approximately ½ in. [1.27cm] thick.

3 Press your object evenly into the molding compound to a depth of between ⅛–¾ in./ 3mm-1.9cm **[3]**. Leave the object in the material until the mold sets. Once the mold has set, lift the object out of the mold. The mold is now ready to be used.

4 Estimate the amount of metal clay needed to fill the mold. Use more clay than you think you'll need. Grease your plastic mat and roller, then roll the clay out to just a little larger than the impression. Put the clay on top of the mold and roll it, pressing the clay into the crevices of the mold **[4]**.

5 Carefully remove the clay from the mold **[5]**. The easiest method is to take your plastic mat and put it on top of the clay, and then turn everything upside down, pulling away the mold and letting the mat support the clay impression.

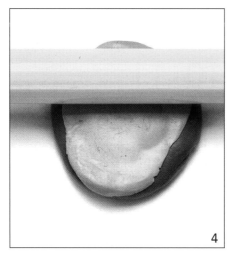

materials

- item to make a mold from
- PMC+ or PMC3 lump clay
- PMC+ or PMC3 syringe clay
- casting grain
- 4mm kiln-safe cubic zirconia (CZ)
- two-part molding compound
- anvil or other flat object
- cooking spray
- paper towel
- Badger Balm or olive oil
- roller
- plastic mat
- craft knife or scalpel
- **2** cocktail straws
- tweezers
- small brush
- water
- metal file
- needle stylus
- hotplate
- steel brush
- burnisher
- tumbler (optional)
- liver of sulfur (optional)

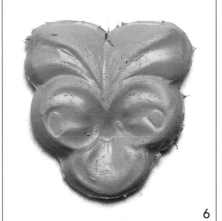

6

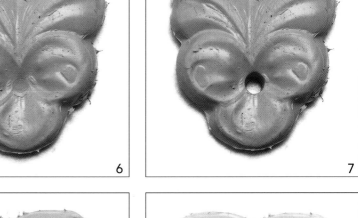

7

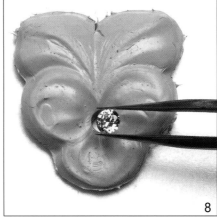

8

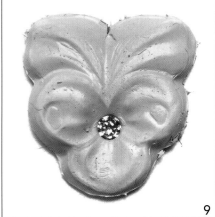

9

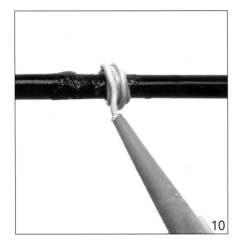

10

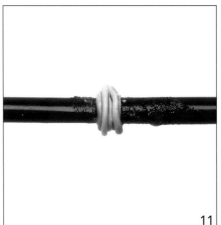

11

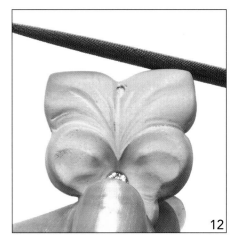

12

6 Use a craft knife to cut away the excess clay **[6]**.

7–9 Take a cocktail straw and punch a hole for the placement of the cubic zirconia (CZ) **[7]**. Use the tweezers to set the CZ on top of the hole **[8]**. Gently push the CZ in with your tweezers. Make certain that the edge of the CZ sinks below the level of the clay **[9]**.

10–11 Take a cocktail straw, grease it liberally, and create a bail with syringe clay by wrapping a syringe-clay tail around the straw until you have achieved the width you want **[10–11]**. Let the bail and the pendant dry thoroughly.

12 Very carefully, use a metal file on the sides of the bail and make certain that the hole is clear of filings and sharp edges. Then use the metal file to smooth the edges of the pendant **[12]**; the amount of detail along the edges of the piece will determine the amount of filing. Depending on how far you pushed the object into the molding compound, you may want to use the filing to contour the edges and create more detail. If you are planning on signing your piece, do so now using a needle stylus.

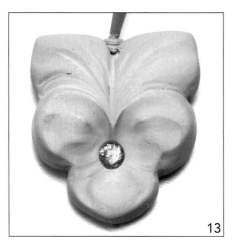

13

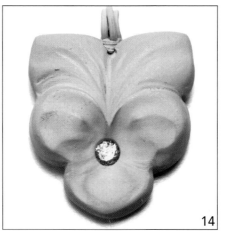

14

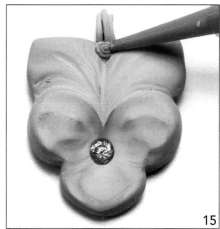

15

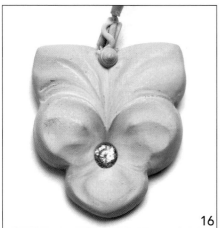

16

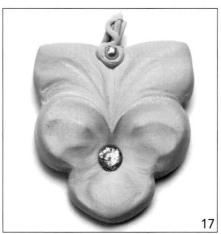

17

18

19

13–17
Wet both the bail and the pendant, then attach the bail to the rest of the piece with syringe clay [13–14]. To make the connection stronger, use syringe clay liberally, and put an extra blob of syringe clay at the base of the bail [15-16]. Embellish the bail by putting a piece of casting grain into the blob [17]. If you wish, reinforce the bail with a bit more syringe clay. Let the piece dry completely overnight, or hasten its drying using a hotplate.

18–19
Fire the piece according to the manufacturer's instructions. Scrub the piece with a steel brush and polish it with a burnisher until the silver shines [18]. If you have a tumbler, you can use that instead. If you wish, use liver of sulfur to add a patina [19] as described on page 19.

Embellished bracelet

Stack flat shell beads on textured
metal clay links and secure them
in place with wire spirals. If
you enjoy this technique, turn
to page 93 for additional
project ideas.

This design, one of my earliest ones, was created after I developed the technique of embedding wire in metal clay. As a beader, I was eager to incorporate beads into my metal clay pieces, and these flat, hand-carved shell flower beads worked perfectly for these bracelet links. I've continued making variations on this project; see page 93 for more examples.

Be sure to use fine silver for the embedded wire; any other type of silver will blacken during firing.

1 Cut the fine-silver wire into five segments of 15–20mm each (the bigger the segment, the bigger the spiral you will eventually create in the center of your flower). With your chainnose pliers, grasp 1–2mm at one end of each wire firmly and bend to a 90-degree angle while squeezing the pliers to flatten the wire **[1]**.

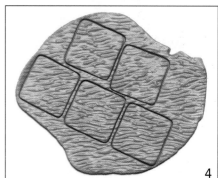

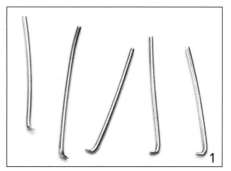

2–3 Grease your texture sheet and roller, then roll the lump clay out to a thickness of four cards on top of the texture sheet **[2]**. Grease your plastic mat and place it on the smooth side of the rolled-out clay. Remove the cards and carefully flip over the plastic mat, the clay, and the texture sheet; remove the texture sheet **[3]**.

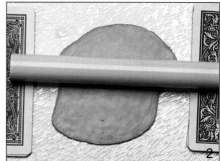

4–5 Using either a craft knife or a clay cutter, cut or punch out five squares that measure approximately 20×20mm **[4]**. Remove the excess clay around the shapes **[5]**.

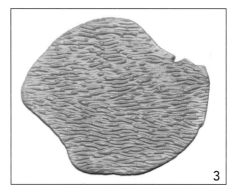

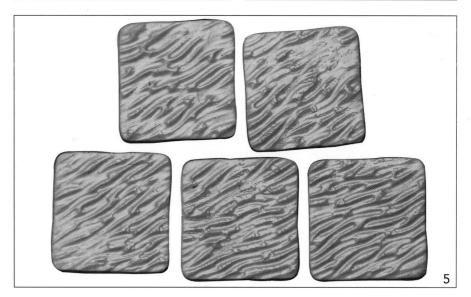

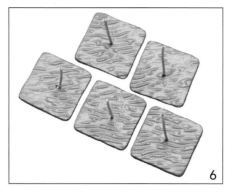

6

7

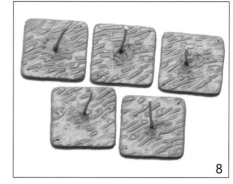

8

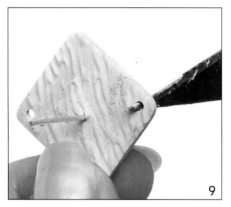

9

10

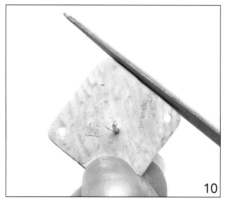

11

12

13

6–7 Embed the flattened, L-shaped end of a wire into each square, making certain the wire doesn't go all the way through the clay to the other side **[6]**. Squeeze a tiny blob of syringe clay at the base of each wire. With a clean, wet brush, flatten the blob around each base **[7]**.

8 With the needle stylus, mark two opposite corners on each square for connecting the links together in a later step **[8]**. Mark the holes approximately 3mm from the edge. Do not create the appropriately sized hole at this stage—only mark the spot for now. Let the squares dry.

9–10 When all shapes are dry, the holes that were begun earlier with the needle stylus will need to be widened. Insert the tip of a craft knife into each hole carefully; hold it at a right angle to the piece and rotate the knife without applying pressure **[9]**. Turn the piece over and repeat so that the hole is even on both sides. Repeat for all the remaining holes. Next, the edges need to be filed until they are smooth **[10]**. Do not touch the wires, even after the pieces are dry; the wires can be easily dislodged at this stage. If you want to sign your piece, do so now using a needle stylus, being very careful not to touch the wires.

materials

- PMC+ or PMC3 lump clay
- PMC+ or PMC3 syringe clay
- 3–4 in. [7.62-10.16cm] 22-gauge fine-silver wire
- 5 flat shell flowers, 8–12mm in diameter
- 22-gauge half-hard sterling-silver wire
- toggle clasp
- Swarovski crystals to complement shell flowers
- wire cutters
- chainnose pliers
- Badger Balm or olive oil
- texture sheet
- roller
- playing cards
- plastic mat
- craft knife or scalpel
- clay cutter (optional)
- small brush
- water
- needle stylus
- metal file or emery board
- steel brush
- burnisher
- liver of sulfur (optional)
- roundnose pliers

14

15

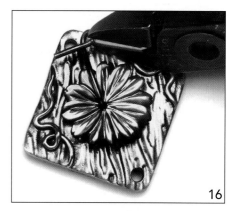

16

17

18

11 Embellish your pieces with syringe clay **[11]**. Let the pieces dry completely.

12–13 Fire the piece according to the manufacturer's instructions. Scrub the piece with a steel brush and polish it with a burnisher until the silver shines **[12]**; exercise care around the wires. If you wish, use liver of sulfur to add a patina **[13]** as described on page 19.

14–18 String a flat shell flower on a wire, right side up **[14]**. With roundnose pliers, make a loop in the wire **[15]**. Use your chainnose pliers to bend the wire into a spiral **[16–18]** to hold the flower in place. Repeat, adding a flat shell bead to each fired piece.

19 Cut a piece of 22-gauge wire and make the first half of a

wrapped loop (see pages 20-21 for wireworking instructions) at one end. Slide one half of the clasp onto the loop and complete the loop. String a crystal onto the wire, make the first half of a wrapped loop, slide the loop through one of the bracelet links, and finish the wraps. Continue until all five links have been connected with wrapped loops and crystals; finish by adding the other half of the clasp **[19]**.

tip

You can experiment with adding various beads to this type of piece. Choose any type of flat, one-sided bead with a hole in the middle.

19

Paint stamped silver clay elements with PMC Gold paste to emulate the texture and color of ancient coins. If you enjoy this technique, turn to page 94 for additional project ideas.

Ancient coins, often composed of more than one metal, were made in a variety of shapes. They feature hundreds of different textures and images—some clear, some mysterious, but all with lots of character. I think of these two-tone, textured earrings as my "ancient coin" project.

This project is the only one in this book that requires torch firing. During firing, the piece should glow medium-orange; if it begins to look too "shiny," hold the torch farther away until the glow returns.

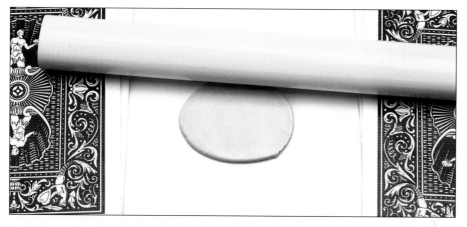

Make paste out of PMC Gold by adding water and letting the mixture stand for several hours.

1 Grease your plastic mat and roller, then roll the lump clay out to a thickness of six cards [1]. Set the clay aside, covered in cling wrap to retain moisture.

2 Spray the stamp with cooking spray and remove the excess oil with a paper towel. Subtract two cards from each stack, for a total of four cards in each stack. Place the stamp face up between the cards, being certain to rest the cards on the edges of the stamp. Place the clay on top of the stamp with the cards framing it on both sides; roll over the clay to make the imprint [2].

3 Carefully remove the clay from the stamp and place the clay on the plastic mat, imprinted side up [3].

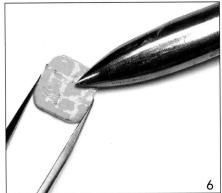

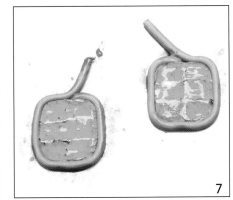

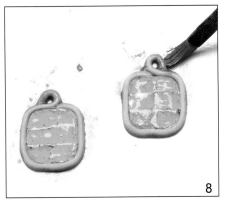

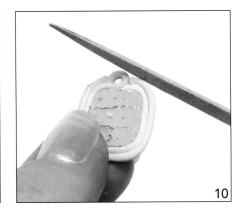

4 Using a craft knife or scalpel, cut two shapes out of the clay, approximately 15×15mm in size **[4]**. Let the pieces dry. Use a metal file or an emery board to smooth the edges on both pieces. If you are planning on signing your pieces, do so now using a needle stylus.

5 Using a clean brush, apply the gold paste to each square **[5]**. Wait for the pieces to dry thoroughly and apply another layer. Let the pieces dry again.

6 Fire the pieces for three to four minutes using a torch. Burnish the pieces while still hot, holding them on the sides with tweezers **[6]**.

7–9 Using the syringe clay without the tip, start in the middle of one side of a square and follow the outline of the piece closely until you get back to the starting point; leave a tail of about 12mm **[7]**. With a wet brush, make a loop out of the tail and attach it to the syringe-clay frame **[8]**. Then apply a second line of syringe clay, starting at the base of the loop and ending on the other side of the same loop **[9]**. Use a wet brush to shape the frame. Now follow these same steps for the other square, except apply the syringe clay in the opposite direction on this piece, so that the squares are mirror images of one another. Let the pieces dry thoroughly.

10–11 Once both pieces have dried, use a metal file along the edges **[10]** and across the syringe-clay frame **[11]**.

tip

Use a burnisher to burnish the gold overlay onto the silver shortly after firing, while the piece is still hot. (Use the tweezers to hold onto the piece, so you don't burn your fingers.) This will assure that the gold bonds with the silver.

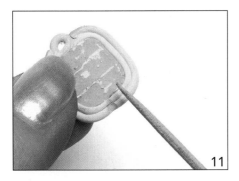

11

12

13

14

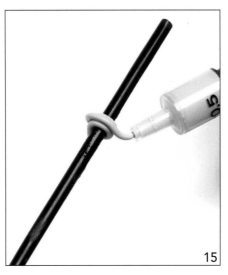

15

materials

- PMC3 lump clay
- PMC3 syringe clay
- PMC Gold paste
- **2** French hook ear wires
- 5-6 in. [12.7-22-gauge half-hard sterling-silver wire
- assorted silver and gold-filled beads, 2–6mm in size
- Badger Balm or olive oil
- plastic mat
- roller
- **12** playing cards
- unmounted stamp (regular thickness, not extra-heavy)
- cooking spray
- paper towel
- craft knife or scalpel
- metal file or emery board
- needle stylus (optional)
- two small brushes (one for silver, one for gold)
- torch
- burnisher
- tweezers
- steel brush
- tumbler (optional)
- liver of sulfur (optional)
- roundnose pliers
- chainnose pliers
- wire cutters
- cocktail straw

12–13 Fire the piece according to the manufacturer's instructions for the syringe clay. Scrub the piece with a steel brush and polish it with a burnisher until the silver shines **[12]**. If you have a tumbler, you can use that instead. If you wish, use liver of sulfur to add a patina **[13]** as described on page 19.

14 To assemble the earrings, cut a piece of 22-gauge wire. Make a wrapped loop (see pages 20-21 for wireworking instructions) at one end and string beads onto the wire as desired. Make the first half of a wrapped loop at the wire end, slide on one of the fired pieces, and complete the loop. Open the loop (see pages 20-21) on an ear wire, slide the dangle onto the loop, and close the loop. Make the second earring to match the first **[14]**.

15 If you wish, make beads to match your earrings. Simply wrap syringe clay around a greased cocktail straw **[15]**, let it dry, remove it from the straw, and fire. For smaller beads, use a toothpick, but there's no need to remove the toothpick before firing. If you have any remaining gold paste, coat the beads and fire as directed above.

Beaded ring

Crystals and Charlottes add sparkle to a syringe clay ring. If you enjoy this technique, turn to page 95 for additional project ideas.

This ring, a recent project, evolved as I searched for even more ways to use beads in my metal clay pieces. Crystals are among my favorite beads to work with, and I think their color and sparkle are perfect for rings. I prefer this piece without a patina, so the shine of the silver can complement the twinkling crystals.

1 Measure your finger to determine your ring size. Because of shrinkage, you will make the ring two sizes larger than the actual size. Wrap a piece of paper around the appropriate size on the step ring mandrel. Wind tape around the paper until the entire piece is covered. Grease the tape liberally **[1]**.

2 Remove the cap from the syringe clay and do not put on the tip. Make two parallel syringe-clay rings around the mandrel about ¼ in. [10mm] apart **[2]**.

3–4 Preshape the brass screen so that it slightly curves to mimic the curve of the mandrel. Place it on top of the two rings of syringe clay on the mandrel **[3]**. Press the edges halfway into the syringe clay **[4]**.

5 Using a very wet brush, manipulate and shape the syringe-clay rings so that they meet on the side opposite from the screen **[5]**.

6–7 Use syringe clay to fill in the triangular gaps at the sides of the screen. Make certain to cover the jagged edges of the screen. You can use the syringe clay with or without the tip for this step. Embellish with cubic zirconias (CZs)

tip

Seed bead selection

When choosing seed beads for needle and thread projects, make certain that the holes in the seed beads are large enough to accommodate the needle and thread passing through them more than once.

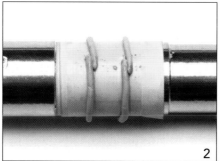

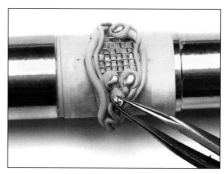

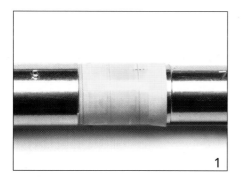

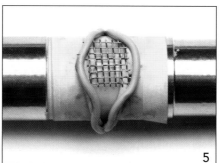

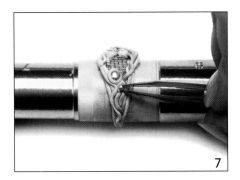

7

8

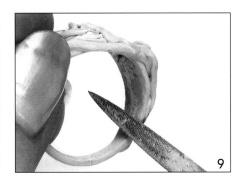

9

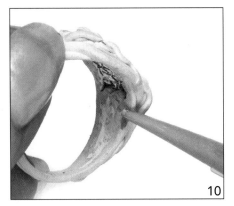

10

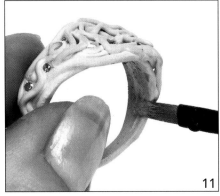

11

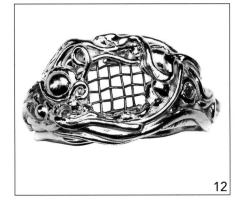

12

materials

- PMC+ or PMC3 syringe clay
- brass screen, ¼ in. [10mm] square
- **6** 2mm kiln-safe cubic zirconias (CZs)
- casting grain
- Superlon or Fireline
- size 13 silver Charlottes
- assorted 4mm Swarovski bicone crystals
- piece of paper, 1×3 in. (2.54x7.62cm)
- step ring mandrel
- tape
- Badger Balm or olive oil
- small brush
- water
- tweezers
- ring mandrel rests
- sanding pads
- metal files
- HattieS Pattie in desired ring size (optional)
- beading needle, size 13

and casting grain by first creating a blob with syringe clay and then using a tweezers to press the CZ or casting grain into the blob **[6–7]**.

8 Dry the piece on the mandrel, putting the mandrel on the ring mandrel rests **[8]**.

9–11 When the ring is dry, take it off the mandrel and remove the piece of paper. Use sanding pads and metal files to smooth the ring so there are no sharp edges on either the inside or the outside **[9]**. Check for any gaps in the syringe-clay work on the inside of the ring. Put the tip on your syringe and fill any gaps **[10]**. Use a wet brush to push syringe clay carefully into the spots that need to be filled **[11]**. Dry the piece again and check for any spots that need

filing or filling; refine as necessary. Pay careful attention to the inside of the ring, making it as smooth as possible for a comfortable fit.

12 Fire according to the manufacturer's instructions. If you are using a HattieS Pattie, fire with the HattieS Pattie in the ring; once the piece is fired, follow the instructions for removal of the HattieS Pattie. Scrub the piece with a steel brush and polish it with a burnisher until the silver shines **[12]**. If you have a tumbler, you can use that instead.

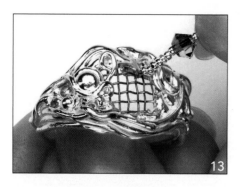

13–14 Cut 3–4 ft. [2.7–3.6m] of beading

thread (Fireline or Superlon is recommended). Tie the thread to the brass screen at the very edge, making two or three knots to secure it. Leave approximately ¼ in. [10mm] of thread after the knot. Thread a size 13 beading needle and secure the end of the thread so it does not slip out of the needle. String five Charlottes, a bicone, and another Charlotte [13]. Go back through the bicone and the first five Charlottes and through the screen [14]. Bring the needle up through the next square of the screen. Keep repeating the process until you have gone all the way around the edge; this completes the first row. Make a total of two or three outer rows, using the same pattern, and going in and out of the same square two or three times. Add more thread as needed.

15 For the next two or three rows, use the same pattern.

As you get closer to the ring's center, decrease the number of Charlottes to three or four, still going two or three times in and out of each square. Once you have completed these rows, fill in the center of the ring where necessary, decreasing the number of Charlottes to one or two, until the ring looks full [15].

16 Tie a knot close to the mesh, and bring the thread through

one of the beaded strands toward the top. Trim the excess thread [16].

Create a cone by piercing a triangular cork core all the way through, just as if you were making a bead.

To make an opening in the side of the vessel, use a straw to punch a hole in the cork clay while it is still moist.

Make vessels with or without handles. You can use a handle to suspend a vessel from a beaded strand. A vessel without handles can be surrounded by beads as well.

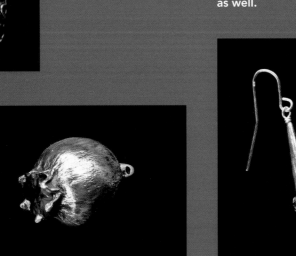

The cubic zirconia in this piece was added after firing, and the piece was then fired again.

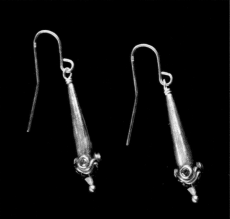

Cover the ends of wooden skewers with paste to create cones for earrings. The wood will burn away when the piece is fired.

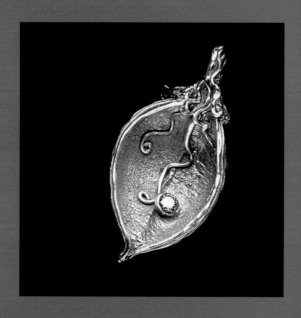

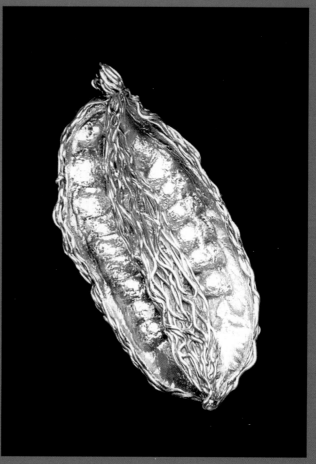

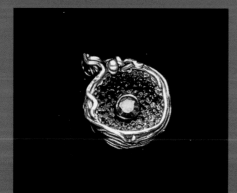

Vary pod types and sizes, cubic zirconia placement, and amount of syringe clay embellishment for a wonderful variety of organic pendants.

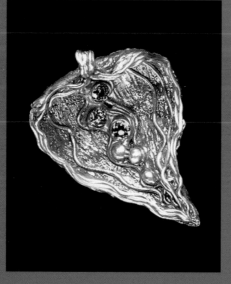

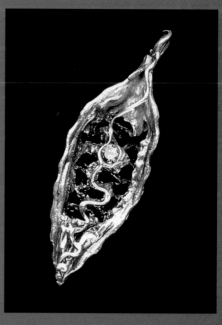

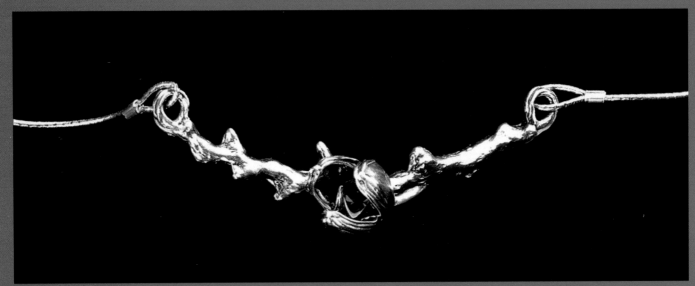

The centerpiece for this necklace was made by combining components from two different plants: a twig and a seedpod. For this type of piece, paint the entire outside of the component.

Use small pods to create matching earrings.

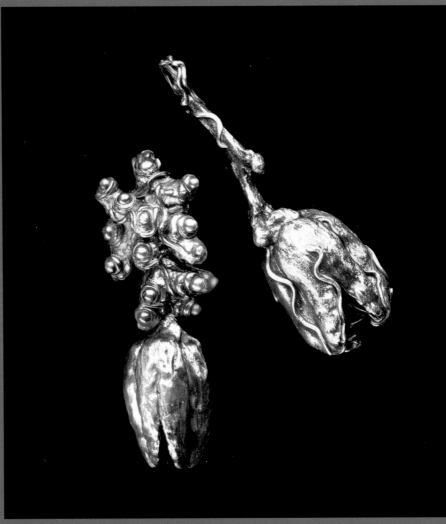

Mix and match pods and other natural forms for memorable pieces. The upper part of the piece at left is yucca, while the lower part is daylily.

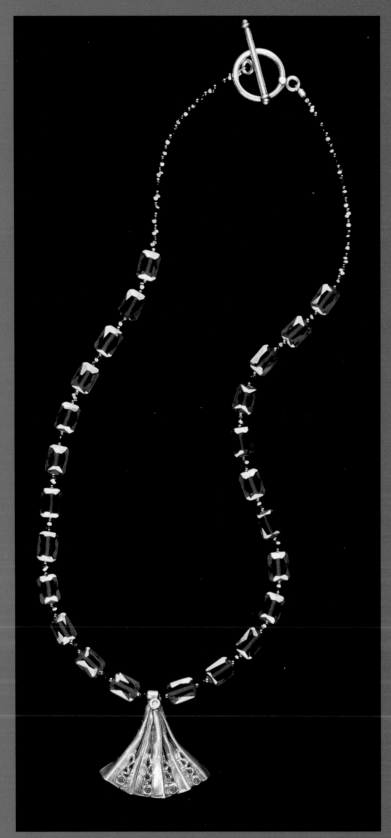

Fold the sheet, then gather and glue one side to create this three-dimensional fan pendant.

If you wish, you can embellish your kimono pendant with syringe clay, like the one at right. Be sure to use water very sparingly when working with sheet clay.

Use paper punches and scrapbooking scissors with a decorative edge to create whimsical, fun pieces like these earrings.

Make bracelet links by creating loops with syringe clay on both sides of the cabochon.

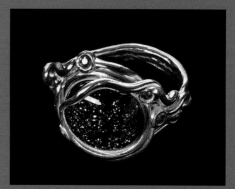

Use the technique shown on page 91 to create a ring. Substitute a dichroic cabochon for the brass screen.

Create earrings by adding small loops on both sides of the cabochon. Be sure to make the earrings mirror images.

Make small charms for earrings and necklaces by punching out a hole with a cocktail straw. The hole will shrink consistently with the rest of the piece.

Punch a hole in the bottom of a carved pendant to create a dangle.

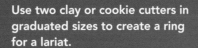

Use two clay or cookie cutters in graduated sizes to create a ring for a lariat.

Metal clay for beaders   **91**

If you are using a large CZ, use an X-Acto knife or scalpel to cut an opening large enough to accommodate it.

Use a shell or a fossil to create a mold.

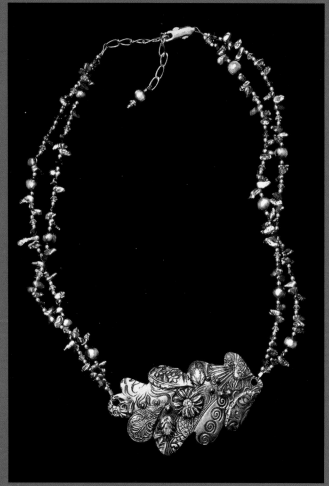

Use molds in conjunction with other textures to achieve a collage effect.

Create earrings to match the pendant on page 70. Use the same mold with PMC Standard for earrings that are much smaller than the pendant.

Create matching earrings by using the same mold twice.

Use the technique described on page 72 to make brooches by attaching pin backs to the findings before firing. Texture the brooches with stamps.

Make chandelier earring components by placing holes accordingly.

Create a centerpiece for a necklace by making holes in the top two corners of a piece.

Stack multiple carved flowers to give this ring a three-dimensional effect.

Use a mold with PMC Gold and fire the piece. Then build the rest of the piece around the fired gold piece to create a two-toned pendant.

Apply several layers of Aura 22 to syringe work to create these earring components.

Use Aura 22 instead of PMC Gold paste to achieve a lighter gold tone.

Use the syringe technique from page 82, replacing the brass screen with a large cubic zirconia, to create these jeweled rings.

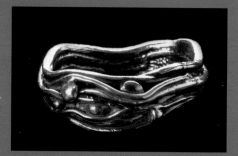

Use the technique on page 82 without the brass screen to create simple rings accented by casting grain.

Create a flower pendant with a brass screen center. Attach a pin back or bail to the back.

Create this cuff bracelet component on a curved mandrel. A plastic bottle or soft drink can will also work.

Resources

Metal clay products and information are available from a wide variety of sources. Here are some that I recommend.

Eclectica, Inc.
Galleria West Shopping Center
18900 W. Bluemound Road, #142-148
Brookfield, WI 53045
262-641-0910
www.eclecticabeads.com

and

The Bead Studio
Galleria West Shopping Center
18900 W. Bluemound Road, #139
Brookfield, WI 53045
262-641-0961

My store, Eclectica, carries beads from around the world as well as all of the PMC products, tools, and accessories you will need to make the projects in this book. We provide a wide variety of beading and metal clay classes. The Bead Studio offers beading kits, studio time and tool rental, kiln-firing services, and space for private parties.

PMC Connection
3718 Cavalier Drive
Garland, TX 75042
866-762-2529
www.pmcconnection.com

PMC Connection sells a full range of PMC products, tools, and accessories. The Web site also provides a listing of teachers and senior teachers nationwide. If you are interested in certification, use the site to look for certification workshops in your area.

Beadissimo
1051 Valencia Street
San Francisco, CA 94110
415-282-2323
www.beadissimo.com

This San Francisco store sells PMC products, tools, and accessories. Their comprehensive class schedule includes beading, wirework, and PMC classes, as well as traditional metalworking and glass beadmaking.

The Bead Factory
3019 6th Avenue
Tacoma, WA 98406
888-500-BEAD
www.thebeadfactory.com

This 5,000-square-foot store carries thousands of beads, PMC products and tools, and other jewelry-making items. Their classes cover everything from basic beading and wirework to PMC and glass beadmaking.

Byzantium
1088 North High Street
Columbus, OH 43201
888-291-3130
www.bigbead.com

This Ohio store carries beads and PMC products as well as textiles, finished jewelry, candles, cards, and stationery.